THE BEHAVIOR SAVIOR

The Enlightened Path to the Perfect Pet

By

Dina Zaphiris

PHOENIX
BOOKS

Library of Congress Cataloging-in-Publication Data

Zaphiris, Dina, 1970-
 The behavior savior : the enlightened path to the perfect pet / Dina Zaphiris.
    p. cm.
 ISBN 978-1-60747-757-0 (pbk.)
 1. Dogs--Training. 2. Dogs--Behavior. I. Title.
 SF431.Z37 2010
 636.7'0835--dc22
                            2010006204

Cover Design and Book Design by Marti Lou Critchfield

Printed in the United States of America

Phoenix Books, Inc.
9465 Wilshire Boulevard, Suite 840
Beverly Hills, CA 90212

10 9 8 7 6 5 4 3 2 1

"All knowledge, the totality of all questions and all
answers, is contained in the dog."

—*Franz Kafka*

For Richard Vye
Who inspired me to train dogs, and forever changed my life

Table of Contents

Introduction

Oh. I get it. If I yell at you, growl in your face like a dog, poke you, talk in a dominant tone, and maybe even flip you over on your back, you'll listen.

Ever had a boss, teacher, or parent try to yell at you or "discipline" you into doing something? How would it feel to be "dominated" by an alpha who showed you who was boss all the time? Most people, and animals, do not thrive in or learn from that kind of environment. In fact, it usually creates lack of trust, bond, mutual respect, and partnership—the qualities that great relationships are based on, both human and animal. Bullying someone really doesn't work. Do you scream and yell at your children and threaten them into doing what you'd like them to do? You're only breaking the trust and bond, respect and cooperation that you desire, and you risk creating a rebel child at the same time.

What about working for free? Yes, really. Go to work for a week, and at the end of the week I'm not going to pay you anymore. No paycheck. I'm just going to say, "Good girl! That's my girl!" I guarantee you, it's not enough to keep you going back to work. Praise is not enough. Using food as a reward can be one of the most important things you do with your dog. It's scientifically proven to help the dog repeat and retain behaviors. No one works for free. Neither should our pets. The trick is to understand intermittent reinforcement so that food can be used less and less once your dog understands what you'd like him to do. Have you ever tried to discipline a grizzly bear? Neither has a zookeeper or any expert in wild animal behavior, and for a darn good reason. You'll get killed. What about putting a tight leash on a bottlenose dolphin or killer whale? Probably won't work. How about flipping a tiger over on his back to show him who's boss? Yet, dolphins in the Navy Marine Mammal Program, also known as military dolphins, are trained using positive reinforcement to detect dangerous underwater sea mines with their sonar.

What about the amazing working dogs? The ones who guide the blind, find missing persons in the wilderness, detect bombs or narcotics at airports, and guard our nation's borders? What about the dogs that detect cancer scent in human breath, or detect an oncoming seizure? The near perfection of the working dog is a perfect example of animals trained with positive reinforcement and marker signals. We can use drive-building games and positive reinforcement to get the best-behaved dogs in the world, yet today our pet dogs are suffering and being disciplined into behaving.

Operant conditioning has been around since the 1800s, yet few people pay attention to it. Operant conditioning is the means by which an animal interacts with his environment to get what he wants and needs. We can actually manage and control a dog's environment so that the dog will *choose* behaviors that we see as desirable. Rather than forcing the dog to do what we want, we set up the environment so the dog can choose and then be reinforced for making the right choice. This is the best way to teach your dog.

Right now, however, our nation's model of dog training preaches discipline as the main model—and the only way—to train your dog. There's this myth that you have to be more dominant and that you even have to use punishment. I keep hearing, "Just dominate," or, "Be the leader, the pack leader." Well, it doesn't work. In fact, science has shown that discipline and correction-based training can lead to an aggressive dog that lacks trust and could one day even try to defend himself against you. Training with correction or punishment creates a fearful dog, one who listens because he has to listen, not because he wants to listen. A dog who wants to listen is the trainable, willing partner we seek to create. Wild animals, zoo animals, and domestic working dogs can be trained to do incredibly complex behaviors with the use of positive reinforcement, yet the only animals we punish and discipline, flip over, yell at and jab, hit, and maybe even kick or swat with a newspaper…are our pet dogs. Your dog will not magically listen if he believes you are the leader. You still need to train him on what to do.

Consequences drive behavior. A consequence can be good. When we look at our pet dogs and begin to understand where the reinforcement lies, we begin to understand why some behaviors "work" for the dog. Dogs repeat behaviors that get them exactly what they want. Simply ask yourself, "What's the reinforcement here? What's my dog getting out of this?" It can be a very powerful question.

Most all other animals that humans work with, from movie dogs to sheep herding dogs, are trained using the methods of operant conditioning and positive reinforcement. Even cattle going into the chute used to be prodded with a hot poker, but the amazing Temple Grandin came along and simply saw things from the cow's point of view, saving the nation billions of dollars in time and energy and creating "willing" cattle, using *no* punishment or discipline to get the cattle into the chute. By making it a positive experience for the cattle, they were more and more willing to go in. Grandin recognized that cattle were frightened to go through the chute because of reflections in puddles, light issues, and the added association of being prodded with a hot poker. When the cow saw the chute, he knew he was about to be prodded, and it created more stress and anxiety for the poor cow. How does discipline like this affect a cow the next time he's supposed to go into a chute? It doesn't work.

Using punishment with a dog does not work, either. Even cattle we handle with positive reinforcement and without discipline, yet our pet doggies are suffering. If punishment, correction, and discipline make up the model of training, the dog will exhibit learned helplessness, and he will lead a life filled with fear and anxiety. The nation needs a new model for dog training. Through the use of positive reinforcement and marker signals, we can create a loving dog that actually understands what we want. We can create a loving, bonded, and respectful partnership with our dogs. We can have a dog that loves to listen, not one who listens out of fear.

Why this book?

This book is a manual, a guide to enhance your relationship with your dog. It touches on training, health, psychology, games, mental stimulation, and what a dog needs in order to be happy. Yes, a happy dog is a good dog. You will be happier if your dog is happy.

I do not focus on training dogs to "sit," "down," or "stay" in this book. It's covered in some detail, but it's not the core of this book. In fact, the guidelines and understanding you learn in this book will make it possible for your dog to learn the basic obedience commands with passion and vigor.

This book is about bonding, partnership, and the true understanding of your dog. He needs you to understand him. All dogs sit. They all lie down, too. I've never seen a dog who doesn't "sit" and "down." Why would we focus on teaching the dog something he already knows? They all "sit" and "down" and "stay" all day long. Just observe them, and you'll see. What is about to follow in this book makes "sit" and "down" seem like meaningless kibble in a world full of filet mignon. "Sit" and "down" do not make a good dog. *Much* more important in shaping a good, well-rounded dog are the consequences (both good and bad) that follow a behavior (such as jumping, barking, sitting, or coming). In no way will understanding "sit" or "down" create a good dog—but the information in this book will. After reading this book, you'll be ready to begin basic "obedience" work with your dog.

The amazing part about this book is that it's human. My lessons with clients and their dogs over the past fifteen years have been more about "correcting" problems that already exist. If only my clients had known what they were doing wrong! When humans realize that they have created all the problems within their dogs' behavior, it brings up frightening territory in their own lives. Maybe they've never set a boundary, have never been able to say "no," or have no idea of the power of positive reinforcement. Maybe they can't control their own children, lives, and work. I've always wondered why there wasn't a manual on how to raise children. Some kind of required instruction book about how they work.

Stop making the mistakes that will mess up your dog—and possibly your children, spouse, employees, and life—forever. Read on and learn how to better your life through understanding the canine mentality. I guarantee you, when you apply these themes to your own life, you'll be amazed. You'll get what you want every time you ask. You just have to be willing to listen… to your dog, and to yourself.

The "perfect" pet

Ok…are you ready? The "perfect" pet is *your* pet. Your dog is perfect. The enlightened path teaches us that we have the *exact* pet we need at certain points in our lives. Our pets are here to teach us things, as we are here to teach them. Perfection is being able to communicate clearly with your dog. Of course, in life, there really is no perfection. We can, however, approximate it by creating a loving, bonded partnership with our beloved dogs. After reading this book, you will realize that *your* dog is the perfect pet.

—The Behavior Savior

A WORD ON REAL AGGRESSION

If your dog has injured another dog or person, this book is not for you. Your dog has an aggression problem, and you need to work with an experienced behavior specialist. This book is for the prevention of bad habits and for the friendly social dog to learn and communicate with you. These methods should not be used with a truly aggressive dog.

Chapter 1

Building Relationship and Bond

Behaviors can be changed, dominance cannot

If you saw me on my worst day, at my worst moment, on the freeway with a car cutting me off and almost killing me, you may call me aggressive. I am not an aggressive or dominant person, but in that exact moment I seemed like an extremely violent and aggressive person. I simply had an aggressive moment.

The mistake people make with their dogs is that they label them as aggressive or dominant, when really they may have only had a moment of aggression. When we label our dogs, it's very hard to treat the label. Labels can't be treated; only behaviors can be treated and changed. A *personality* trait, such as dominant, can't be changed. When we label our dogs as dominant, it often leaves us feeling like we must be *more* dominant in order to show them who's boss. This is simply ridiculous. Instead, concentrate on the specific behavior you'd like to change, and use training and positive reinforcement to change it. Behaviors can be changed, personality traits cannot.

Do not believe you can "fix" a dominant dog. Dominance cannot be "cured." What *can* be treated, however, are behaviors such as mounting other dogs, pulling on the leash, or jumping on people. If your dog has a problem lunging at other dogs when he's on a leash, do not call him aggressive or dominant. Call it a problem lunging on the leash, and work on fixing that specific behavior.

Allowing your dog to do what people call "dominant" things, like sleeping on the bed or going through the door first, in no way affects your dog's behavior in any other area. People seem to think that by not allowing their dogs to sleep on the bed with them, this will change their dogs into thinking that they now have a leader. Wrong. The only thing you're changing is that one specific behavior. Now, you simply have a dog who does not sleep on the bed, which has no bearing on anything else.

Behaviors are specific, and they are our only hope for changing something that is unwanted. If you do not want your dog running out the front door when you open it, then work on fixing *that specific behavior*. People seem to think that by dominating their dogs, it will help change their dogs' behavior. That's simply impossible. Antecedents (what comes before the behavior) do not change behavior. Behavior is driven by consequences—both positive and negative. How does "acting like the alpha" get your dog to come when you call him? It doesn't. It can't. The only thing that can help your dog come when you call him is training him to do so with desirable consequences. Train the behavior you want by reinforcing and rewarding with food and jackpots.

When you act like a dominant leader, your dog will wonder why you're acting so stiff and mean. He'll probably begin to fear you, become confused and anxious, and try to stay away from you. He'll be less likely to come to you and more likely to run away or bolt from someone who seems dominant.

Consequences drive behavior

"Zeus, drop my sock! RIGHT NOW. D-R-O-P. ZEUS!"

I don't think so. Unless you've actually trained your dog to "drop" an object, he really has no idea what you're talking about. I see this all the time. Clients tell me, "He won't come when called," and they've actually never formally trained their dog to "come." It's crazy. If you were in a foreign country and someone was barking orders at you, you wouldn't follow them either—not because you're disobedient or stubborn, but because you have no idea what the person is saying.

Solution

Consequences drive behavior, so providing food reinforcement is very powerful and will build a dog who understands which behaviors are wanted and correct.

Timing is hugely important in dog training. Dogs can't learn after the fact. They learn instantly, in the moment. A great example of how dogs learn is the sneeze trick. You can stand all day and tell your dog to sneeze for you. He'll look at you like you're nuts. Instead, wait for him to sneeze. Have your treats on your waist pouch so that you're always prepared. The very second he sneezes say, "Good sneeze," and point to your nose. Immediately follow with a treat. All of my dogs now sneeze on cue. I had to wait for the sneezes first, then name it and reward it. Soon they began sneezing more and more. I'd be eating a sandwich, and my chow mix Eugene would come over and "sneeze" at me on purpose because he knew that would get him a bite of food! This is called offering. Without ever asking him to sneeze, he began to sneeze more on his own. Now I knew he was ready for the cue. "Sneeze," I said to him after a few days, and he did.

Your dog doesn't understand English unless you teach him what the words mean. Don't expect him to listen to you if you haven't formally trained him.

Dogs learn to exhibit behaviors that you pay attention to. So, wouldn't it make sense to pay attention to your dog when he's just quietly lying on the floor, next to your feet? Pay attention to your dog *before* he acts up. If you're doing your own thing, your dog barks, and you look over at him, you've just rewarded the barking. Eye contact is a reward, so when you give that "don't you bark" look to your dog, you're actually giving him a desired reward: your eyes.

Bond first, train later

Try going up to a complete stranger on the street and asking him to run an errand for you. Be really nice, and just ask. The stranger will look at you like you're completely nuts. He has no reason to listen to you. He does not trust or respect you and is not bonded to you in any way. He doesn't know you enough to like you. Why should he listen to you?

Now go up to someone you know and have a bond with, and ask him to run the same errand for you. You'll see quite different results.

I see people asking their dogs to do things like sit, come, and stay, and the dog completely blows them off. Why? He has no reason to listen to you. And on top of that, he has no idea what you're saying to him or what you want. He doesn't speak English. If you are not bonded properly to your dog, he most likely doesn't understand what you want from him.

Solution

Bond first, then train. Whether your dog is old or young, he will *not* listen to you until you take the time to bond with him. Some great ways to bond with your pup include: spending time together, hand feeding, going on walks and hikes, playing, and understanding what your dog likes and loves. This bonding time forms mutual trust and respect and creates a language between you and your pup. Training your dog also helps to create bond. But you need more than just the training. Your dog wants more from you than just to listen. Create a good bond *first*, and then begin to train.

Set goals

In whatever task you're taking on, it's very important to set goals. A lot of my clients don't really know what they want from their dogs or even what amazing things their dogs are capable of. My dog brings me a beer or water from the fridge, and he carries my bags to the car for me. Really! My Aussie can skateboard on his own board alongside me on mine. The sky is really the limit. But if you don't set goals, you'll probably end up with an inconsistent dog because training him won't be important enough on your list of things to do.

Solution

Set Goals. Write down how your ideal dog would behave. What commands and cues would he know? Would he do tricks? Would he become a therapy dog and visit children's hospitals? If you are clear with your goals, it will help you to better train your dog.

Bond through hand feeding

I'm very big on hand feeding your dog for the first *six to eight weeks* that you have him. I don't mean sometimes—I mean *all* the food comes from your hands. Wash the food bowl, and put it away. Whether he's an eight-week-old pup or a six-year-old rescue, hand feeding can be one of the best ways to bond with your dog. It really teaches him that *you* provide his food. Otherwise, he naturally thinks that his bowl provides his food. He doesn't realize that you work, get a paycheck, cash it, drive to the store, buy him dog food, schlep it home, and then put it in his bowl. He has no way to appreciate it. When you hand feed, you actually show him that you are his food provider. If he eats out of the bowl, chances are he's more bonded to the bowl than he is to you.

Bowl feeding creates a fat, gorging dog, and leaving the food bowl down all day creates a picky eater. If you leave that bowl down, your dog is probably in a perpetual state of fullness. He can't possibly be motivated by treats if you do this, and you'll be stuck using force to train him. Your dog will see food as having little or no value, and he'll become a nibbler, nibbling one or two pieces of kibble each hour or so. You wonder why he's not eating, so then you change the food or "add" chicken or cheese to his food…. No! Do *not* do this. You are creating a picky eater who will lack proper motivation for training and who doesn't get to look forward to mealtimes.

Solution

Whether he's a puppy or an older dog, hand feed your dog for six to eight weeks. Feeding your dog by hand helps create a bonded dog and teaches your dog to become motivated to earn food. We all have to work for our food. This gives us value as a person, and meaning. Well, dogs have to work for their food too.

It gives them something to do and look forward to, and it can be really rewarding. You are your dog's coach. A great coach can relate to his team, giving wonderful examples and engaging the team members. This is what creates team spirit and wins games. If you do not have team spirit, or bond, with your dog, he will not listen to you.

Science and research has, after all these years, come back to say that there's actually no alpha wolf in the "pack." In fact, L. David Mech, the very man who coined the phrase "alpha" and has done more research than anyone in this field, has come back to say he made a mistake. Wolf groups are based on cooperation, partnership, and the control of resources (hand feeding), which is one of the most important factors. Being the "dominant alpha" is not anywhere near as important as controlling the resources. Wolf packs are based on cooperation and mutual respect. Wolves and wild dogs change rank all the time. Researchers have shown that wolves actually structure their lives much like human families. By controlling all the food, your dog realizes that *all* the resources come from you, and he's much more likely to listen and be motivated to train.

Eventually you will begin training and hand feeding. When training begins, usually on week two of hand feeding, we can begin by training when the dog is hungry and ready to eat. A full dog has no reason to learn anything new. Remember, it's not about starving your dog; he can have his entire daily amount of food. But it's all coming from you. Squat down with your dog's meal in a treat pouch. You can add some yummy treats in as well, but it's important that all his food for the entire day is worn around your waist in a pouch. Barking and jumping may increase in the beginning because you have the pouch on. But as soon as he learns that jumping and begging gets him no food, he'll sit or lie down or try another behavior. When he does a calm, wanted behavior, give him a kibble. Just be sure to feed him as a reward for proper and wanted behaviors, and never feed him for unwanted ones. This exercise helps the dog *not* to beg because he learns that begging never earns him a morsel of food. Make the feeding last all day or do it all at once, depending on how much time you have.

I promise you, the best dogs are hand fed. You will notice that your dog begins to make more eye contact with you because he has to connect with you to receive food. Squat down and say your dog's name as he's eating, over and over again. Soon, you'll ask him for behaviors to receive food, but for now, just squat and feed. As your pup is crunching his meal from one hand, gently stroke his head with your other hand. The sound of your voice, your touch, his name, and the smell of you all become powerful secondary reinforcers through this game. What's a "secondary reinforcer?" Anything that's paired with a primary reinforcer (food) long enough to form an association. Pretty soon, the secondary reinforcers (your voice, the dog's name, your smell) become as powerful, and sometimes even more powerful, than the primary reinforcer. You are creating relationship and bond so that your dog has a reason to "listen" to you down the road.

Eventually, after *six to eight weeks* of hand feeding, you may go back to bowl feeding. And yes, when he's hungry he will eat out of his bowl again. Feed twice a day, and leave food down for fifteen to twenty minutes. That's it. Do *not* give in. If he doesn't eat, he's not hungry. And besides, his next mealtime is in six to eight hours. Big deal. If you stick to a schedule, he'll look forward to mealtimes. Puppies, lactating females, or elderly dogs are exceptions, but a normal, healthy dog should have two separate meals of fifteen to twenty minutes each.

Feeding twice a day helps you learn his potty schedule as well. If he "nibbles" all day, he'll pee and poo all day, which can make potty training very difficult. If he looks forward to mealtimes, you will be able train before the meal because he'll be motivated. Don't give in. He's *not* going to starve himself, I promise.

Creating a "voice marker"

A "voice marker" is a special word and tone, combined with a treat, that tells your dog the exact moment he has engaged in a desired behavior.

Make your voice marker really powerful by playing the following game. Let's use the word "YES!" Stand with a handful of yummy treats, and get your dog excited about them. Hold one in your hand and say, "YES," and pop a treat into his mouth. Repeat. Keep saying "YES" with the same exact tone and excitement in your voice. Give him all the treats, one by one, and say, "YES," before each treat is given. You've just created a powerful secondary reinforcer: the word "YES."

Now ask for a behavior, like eye contact. Say your dog's name, and when he makes eye contact, say, "YES," and immediately follow with a treat. Now try "sit." The instant your dog's rear end hits the floor, say, "YES," and follow with a treat. The word "YES" is like a promise to your dog. It's the promise of a reward. Pretty soon, when your dog has a great understanding that this word is extremely good and valuable, you can start to add more time in between the word "YES" and the delivery of the treat. Your dog, however, has a "marker" that tells him he's doing *exactly* what you want. He will start to "work" to earn his voice marker and reward!

Try running away from your dog and calling him to "come." You can say, "YES," the instant he runs toward you, or you can say, "YES," when he arrives at your feet. Vary it—both are good choices. For potty training, say, "YES," at the exact moment your dog potties in the correct location. Follow with a treat.

What happens when you say, "YES," and have no treat to follow? The "YES" becomes "poisoned" or meaningless. Always have a treat ready if you're going to use your voice marker. Don't fake him out. "YES" is a promise of a treat. Why not *just* reward, with no voice marker? Because your dog probably won't know which behavior you're rewarding. For example, let's say your dog pees on the lawn, and you go inside to give him his treat for peeing outside. Well, by the time you give him the treat, he forgot what behavior you're rewarding. He most likely thinks he gets a treat for coming back inside the house and *not* for pottying. If you say, "YES," when he begins to pee in the outside potty area, then he really understands which behavior is earning him the treat. Bonding is about building clear communication with your dog. A voice marker is a very clear signal to tell your dog the *exact* moment he's doing the right thing.

Try teaching "go to your bed." Start off by throwing yummy treats onto his dog bed. When he jumps on the dog bed to eat the treats, say, "YES." Then run away so he'll chase you. Repeat. Throw another treat on the bed as you say, "Go to your bed." And then say, "YES," as soon as he touches the bed. Now see if he'll "go to his bed" without you throwing the treat. If he does, follow with "YES" and throw the treat *after* he goes to his bed. "Go to your bed" is a great way to practice timing and voice marker. Use your voice marker for all correct responses. Eventually, your dog should be able to do three to ten things before earning his "YES." Keep him wondering which behavior will win him the "YES" and the treat. This keeps it really fun, interesting, and exciting for your dog.

Create time for bonding

It's simple: if you don't have time for a dog, do not get a dog.

Solution

Make time for your dog. You need to spend quality time with your dog to create bond. What's enough time? Depending on breed, age, and personality, you should spend *at least* an hour a day one-on-one with your dog. And watching TV does *not* count. Two thirty-minute walks, an hour in the dog park, three twenty-minute training sessions—usually this is the minimum requirement for a dog. If you work for twelve hours a day, the dog may not be the right pet for you at this time in your life. If you have a houseful of people, work at home, or have a dog walker, maybe it's a possibility. Really think about if you have enough time for a dog.

You are your dog's trainer

Do you really think your dog will listen to you, trust you, bond with you, become your partner, and respect you if *someone else* trains him? Training is built on bonding and relationship. If you send your dog away to be trained, he'll bond with someone else. He's not going to listen to you when he gets home from camp. Sometimes the dog will listen when he first gets home, but his obedience will gradually deteriorate over time…and meanwhile, you never learned how to train your dog.

Solution

Work with a trainer to help *you* train your dog. Good dog trainers are training the people, not the dog. You'll be *much* happier in the long run if you take the time out to train with your dog and a trainer. If you don't have the time to train, then you probably don't have time for a dog. The only time I recommend sending the dog away is if the owner follows through and does eight weeks of training with the trainer when he gets home from camp. This can make it easier on the owner because the dog now understands what's wanted of him, and now the owner just has to learn.

Listen to your dog, and he'll listen to you

Is your dog fulfilled? I used to think this sounded funny, but it's actually very important. You shouldn't expect your dog to listen to you when you haven't listened to him.

Solution

Know your breed, his exercise and other needs, and be sure you are fair enough to fulfill his needs before you expect him to "listen" to you in or out of the house.

If your dog has been at home cooped up all day, don't come home and flip on the TV. Your dog will probably drive you mad. Take a walk or throw a ball for fifteen to thirty minutes. Then you can expect him to lie quietly by your side as you watch a movie.

A "good" dog usually has a good relationship and bond with his owner. A bond is a two-way street. There has to be something in it for both involved. This is true for human relationships as well. Haven't you ever had a "one-sided" relationship? Well, it usually doesn't last long, and it certainly isn't any fun. Your dog feels the same way. You need to fulfill his needs, and I guarantee you, he'll fulfill yours.

Welcome your dog into your den

"I can't figure out why Rex is so hyper! We live on twenty acres, and he has *so* much land to run around on all day. He can exercise himself." You don't know how often I hear this one. First of all, dogs do not "exercise themselves." Whether you have one acre or one hundred acres, most likely your dog is sitting by the sliding glass door peering in at you. He's definitely not out running laps on his own, I can guarantee you that. He wants to be with *you*.

Terrible behaviors and habits begin when you leave a dog all day in the backyard. Digging, excessive barking, boundary/fence aggression, compulsive licking…the list goes on and on.

Solution

Teach your dog how to live peacefully inside your home. Go out with him to exercise. Even if you just throw the ball, you need to be there with him. Your dog prefers to live and den with his family group, which is *you*.

Teach your dog what toys are his, and always have access to yummy chew toys in the house. Dogs that are left outside all day tend to act crazy when they're finally let inside. It's a vicious cycle where we end up putting the dog back out again because he's acting hyper. Instead, exercise your dog, and allow him to live in your home. He's a part of the family, and this creates a well-balanced dog.

He should also sleep in your room, either on his own bed on the floor or in a crate. It's also fine for a dog to sleep on the bed with you; it can be cozy on cold nights. In no way does a dog sleeping on your bed create an aggressive or "dominant" dog, which is a myth I hear a lot. In fact, it has nothing to do with how well your dog listens in his everyday life. Listening in everyday life is a result of being rewarded for listening. Sleeping on your bed or not sleeping on your bed has nothing to do with what kind of dog you shape.

Begin training now!

So many bad habits can develop early in a dog's life. Don't let anyone tell you to wait until the pup is six months old. That myth comes from old school–style militant dog trainers who use correction and punishment.

Solution

Start early—as soon as you've started to bond properly with your dog. I begin teaching puppy kindergarten at eight weeks. With positive reinforcement and game training, you can start at eight weeks, as soon as you bring your puppy home.

Start before a problem begins. If you begin training early, you can save a lot of time and money down the road when behavioral issues may develop. Especially if your dog seems "perfect," begin training. You need to establish vocabulary, cues, and rewards. And you need to bond and build your relationship in a consistent manner. Training helps you continue to build this crucial bond. Puppies, like children, hit adolescence and change. Most puppies come when you call them, but when they hit "doggie puberty," this all changes. Suddenly, they do not come when called. Smells, marking, other dogs, squirrels—all become interesting and distracting. This is not a bad thing, but if you establish early recall and training, you can have a dog who understands what these cues mean.

It is so much easier to start teaching basic cues and commands at an early age—just like with humans! We don't wait until we're teenagers to go to school. Rules, boundaries, and training must be established from an early age. An older dog, as long as he is motivated, can learn new behaviors too. It may take a little longer, and you have to be more patient, but when you change your behavior in the proper manner, your dog will follow suit.

Make it fun!

Dogs are like children in so many ways. They need training to be fun. There has to be something in it for them or else it's not worth it, and it's not going to stick.

Solution

Play with your pup! Develop play sessions. It may take you a few minutes to a few days or even weeks to develop good play. This is very important for bonding with your pup.

Sorry guys…. Petting does not count as play. It's a completely different subject. Taking a walk or a hike comes closer, but it's still sometimes not as fun as an all out play session.

Fun is developed through your play relationship. What does your dog think is fun? Find out what your dog *loves*. If you don't know, now is the time to learn. Does he like to chase sticks? Play tug-of-war? Swimming? Hiking? Brisk walks in the morning? Food? You should be able to list ten to twenty food items—treats and human food—in order of importance to your dog.

Fun also translates into "reward" or "positive reinforcement" during training. Eventually, the things he loves will be used as rewards for wanted behaviors. If you know what's fun for your dog, you know how to reward him for a job well done.

GAMES

Some dogs love playing fetch, while some love to swim with you. Figure out what your dog loves to do, and do it with him. See if he loves to play a game, or invent one of your own. Here are a few games that will improve your bond with your dog.

HIDE THE COOKIE

First, start with a treat visible. Tell him to "go find," and let him get the treat. Gradually he'll understand what "go find" means, and you can hide the cookie in more and more difficult locations. Once, I had a Jack Russell terrier search for two hours straight for a cookie I hid in a tree outside. I read a book while he searched and searched. When he found it he couldn't reach it, so I got it down for him. He loved this game more than anything, but he needed me in order to play it with him.

THE "I'M RUNNING AWAY FROM YOU" GAME

This one is very simple. Let your dog "chase" you as if you were live prey. When he "catches" you, let him eat a bite of cheese or tug his favorite toy. Repeat ten times, and you'll lose ten pounds. This will also make your dog use his noggin, which gets him just as tired as exercise. Don't underestimate the power of play.

THE "EYE CONTACT" GAME (AKA SPITTING FOOD)

Stuff your cheeks with cheese or hot dogs. When your dog looks you in the eyes, spit some cheese out at him. I'm serious. It really increases your dog's eye contact and attention. Next, ask for a "sit" or a "come," and spit out his reward. Sure, okay, make sure you're outside in case your dog is not a good "catcher."

This is a really fun way to reward. He'll never know when you're about to spit at him! I keep treats in my mouth during training sessions, and my dog will not break eye contact. Eventually, I'll spit one at him! Reward for longer and longer sustained eye contact. Treat just before you think he's going to be distracted.

See if you can have another dog walk by as you "spit" food. If you practice, your dog would rather look at *you* than the other dog. It's a great way to build attention.

GET THIS THING!

One of my most favorite things to teach my dogs is that I always have the better, more valuable item. I start this game by getting as many toys as I can possibly hold in my arms, and I throw one way out for my dog. He runs after it. As soon as he picks up the toy I just threw, I begin to squeak and run in the opposite direction, saying, "Get this thing! Get this thing!" as I shake one of the toys still in my arms.

This always works. He comes running after me, usually with the other toy in his mouth, and when he gets to me, I throw the new toy *way* out. He chases it, grabs it, and I begin running again, saying, "Get this thing!"

It really teaches the dog that *you* always are more exciting than anything else going on in the world. This is a great tool for hikes and off-leash training. When your dog is after something, or distracted, use the same game (always bring a good tug toy or ball on a hike). Your dog begins to chase a critter, another dog, follow a scent—and you begin to *run* the other way calling, "Get this thing!"

If you practice with *no* distraction and build this game, it's one of the most powerful and fun ways to get your dog to you without using the "come" command. Preserve your "come" command.

This game is also one of the best ways to teach "fetch." Your dog will usually run back to you with the first toy in his mouth. Now you're on your way to fetch, which is simply playing this game with only one toy, instead of five or six. Throw the ball or toy out and say, "Get it!" As *soon* as the dog puts the ball in his mouth, and *no* sooner, call him to you as you run madly away. A perfect fetch is actually a perfect recall! You create a dog who *chooses* to listen to his cues instead of following distractions.

Chapter  2

Socialization

Socialize your dog

This is a big one. Dogs need to be exposed to other dogs and people. Whatever your dog is not exposed to will usually be a source of fear for him down the road. This fear is simply from lack of exposure.

Many people think their dog will turn out normal even if he never gets to see other dogs. This is a myth. This is how fearful and aggressive dogs are created. A dog needs to leave the home and socialize with other dogs, or you risk having a dog that could fight and hurt another dog or one that is fearful of other dogs.

Solution

Begin young. The most critical period for socialization occurs between eight to twenty weeks of age. You must take your dog out during this phase. He should develop into a kind, confident, and unafraid dog. He needs to see balloons and swing sets, people wearing different clothes and glasses, people of all shapes and sizes and colors—this is very important. Would you want to stay home all day and all night, never seeing another person? Well, neither does your dog. He needs to "talk," play, and socialize with his own kind, and with people.

Pups learn from other dogs how to understand, use, and display certain body language and subtle cues from each other. This is extremely important to your dog's development. Usually (not always), an aggressive dog had little or no socialization with other dogs as a pup. Prevent this by taking your dog out. Hikes, walks, play dates, and dog-friendly beaches are all great options. Set up a play date with dogs you know who are very friendly. Owners are usually honest about their dog being aggressive or not. So ask, and don't be afraid.

Even if your family has more than one dog, it is not enough for your pup only to socialize with the other dogs in your backyard. Your pup will learn to like these dogs, but he'll most likely not get along well with other dogs. He needs to meet new dogs all the time. Remember, if you do not socialize your puppy, your puppy will turn out to be the problem dog.

Socialize while you vaccinate

When the dog is between eight and twenty weeks of age, he's going through what's called the socialization period. It is very important for your dog to have many positive experiences during this time. If you want a well-rounded, social, friendly, and healthy dog, you must socialize with other dogs and people and have new and challenging experiences during these crucial twelve weeks.

It's very ironic that the "socialization period" and the "vaccination period" are at exactly the same time in a puppy's life. The vet may try to tell you not to put your puppy on the ground outside and definitely not to meet other dogs. I've heard this from quite a few vets, but the good ones will tell you differently.

Solution

Find safe social situations for your pup. As long as you're socializing with clean, vaccinated dogs, you should be okay. Learn to safely socialize by taking him to clean places. Don't let your puppy eat bird, squirrel, cat, or other dogs' poop. Don't take him to dog parks; they are filled with viruses that can make a puppy very sick. And remember, your puppy can contract a virus or kennel cough if you bring home the virus on your shoes. It's even outside in your lawn. Your pup should be taken immediately to the vet at the first sign of vomit or diarrhea, or refusal of food or water. If you can, have the vet come to your home or even out to your car to vaccinate. The vet office is actually where he could get the sickest. Kennel cough and parvovirus are there because everyone brings their sick dogs to the vet. Do not put your puppy on the floor at the vet's office.

A perfect alternative to dog parks is to have a puppy play date at your house with another clean pup or vaccinated dog. It's very important that he has these early interactions and experiences. If he doesn't, he won't develop socially and could become either fearful or aggressive around things he's never seen or experienced. It's much harder to socialize him later on. Keep in mind, there's a critical window of socialization, but socialization needs to happen throughout your dog's life. He needs to socialize with his own kind, especially in the first twenty weeks. Almost all of the aggressive dogs I treat had improper socialization or no socialization as a puppy. Many of my clients who waited until all vaccines were given before socializing have problem dogs.

Meeting other dogs does not have to mean he's going to be sick. It is dangerous and unhealthy for your dog to be unsocialized. More dogs die each year because of behavioral problems than from infectious diseases. Socialize safely.

HUMAN IMPLICATION

Stop washing your hands with antibacterial soap every five minutes. You are creating a super strong virus by doing this. Relax, and let your kid pick up a stick and eat it. It's really no big deal. Mothers are ultra paranoid about their children. Instead, focus on a healthy diet and keeping immune system defenses up to par. You have a much better chance of getting a cold if you worry all the time. Also, when you really need to say, "No! Don't eat that!" it won't work because you say it all the time in meaningless circumstances.

Relax when greeting another dog

Like a child, your dog looks to you to receive cues on what to do and how to act in new situations. Never let him see you sweat. Your dog can pick up on your feelings. He's actually *smelling* what you are feeling. If you don't "like" someone, your dog will pick up on this. Keep in mind that you give off certain smells (adrenaline, sweat) that your dog easily can sense. We also show our nervousness through our voice, body language, or holding a "tight leash." You're leaving him to decide what to do, and if your dog picks up on this, he will worry that something is terribly wrong.

Solution

Take charge and show by example. When you have a happy, relaxed attitude, this *helps* your dog to follow in suit. Don't wait to see if your dog "likes" the other dog. Jump right in, and immediately begin to pet the other dog and say hello to it in a happy voice. Your dog will see you petting and praising the other dog, pick up on your relaxed, happy energy, and he'll sniff and begin to play or peacefully go his own way. You are taking the initiative to show your dog that this is a friend. This is an important way to keep your dog looking forward to greeting other dogs.

Know the "other" dog. Even if your dog is well behaved, you need to make sure the dog he's about to meet is good, too. If the other dog is barking, growling, and lunging at the end of his leash, do not meet this dog. Talk to people. Ask them, "Is your dog friendly?" They usually tell the truth. Don't leave it up to chance. Look for signs: stiff body language and tail, erect ears, and pulling hard on the leash. These things could mean an out-of-control dog. If your really well-trained, socialized dog meets a dog who is not socialized, he may have to defend himself. This is not your dog's fault. You need to make the call on which dogs to meet and which ones not to meet.

Work with a friend's dog you know your dog loves, and teach him to respond properly in front of this friendly dog first. Of course, if your dog is aggressive, this is not going to work, and you'll need to work with a behavior specialist. Don't go through life with your dog avoiding potential issues. Issues don't magically go away; they get worse.

Avoid greeting mistakes. If you always cross the street when you see another dog coming toward you, this says something very powerful to your dog. He may think something is wrong with other dogs, or learn to fear or avoid other dogs, or it will make him obsessed with other dogs. Why are you crossing the street? Are you scared your dog will bark, lunge, or bite? Instead of crossing the street, work on preventing the problems you don't like. Take food and treats with you on your walk, and start treating your dog like mad every time you see another dog. Soon, your dog will look forward to seeing other dogs, and eventually you can be on the same side of the street.

There is always a way to change your dog's mind and your mind. But you can be sure that if you have an attitude toward something, your dog's attitude usually follows suit. Be careful of what you are signaling to your dogs, or children, for that matter. They pick up on everything. Focus on giving your dog something to *do*. Stop focusing on what *not* to do. Have fun. Lighten up, and relax. Enjoy your dog, and he'll enjoy you.

HUMAN IMPLICATION

Be careful of your fears, moms and dads! My mother taught me fear of flying. Every single time we'd fly, she'd have a full panic attack, cry, and worry. I had to take care of her on the plane. Now, I have tremendous anxiety when I fly. I do it, but that fear from early on is still there. I have no moment of tranquility in the air. Your child looks to you to see how to behave in certain situations. Your behavior is one of the greatest teachers your child may have.

Leave your dog on the ground

Do not pick up your puppy or small dog when you see another dog. This signals to your dog that you are nervous and that something is wrong. Your dog will be frustrated that he can't greet the other dog.

Solution

Let your pup socialize! Ask if the other dog is friendly. If the answer is yes, put your dog down and let him be. If you always pick him up and rescue him, he could become socially underdeveloped and eventually fearful or even aggressive toward other dogs. Let your dog be a dog!

The dog park

I've seen a dog kill another dog at the dog park. It's something I wish I never saw. A man walked into the park with a large male mixed-breed dog. He had just rescued it from the shelter and wanted to see how the dog would do in the park. Unfortunately, within minutes of entering the park, the dog went after a much smaller dog, and the impact alone killed him.

If you are unsure in *any* way whether or not your dog is friendly, do not let him off leash around other dogs. Work with a behavior specialist until you are sure your dog is friendly.

Solution

Spend the first few weeks getting to know your dog. Take leashed walks, and watch his body language when he sees other dogs. Is he wagging his tail with his ears back? Good sign, but it still does not mean he's okay with other dogs. Is he stiff, with his tail erect? Does he stare and growl or bark? These could be signs that your dog is aggressive. Or, it could mean that your dog is just really excited to see the other dog. Do not let your dog off leash to "see" what happens if you're not sure.

Have a well-behaved dog when guests come over

One family I work with has a dog named Ellie. They were afraid of Ellie biting a guest, so they'd lock her in the bedroom every time someone came over. The problem got much worse. Ellie eventually started lunging and snapping at people on the street, too—not just in the home. She associated other people with being locked away from all the family fun.

Sending your dog to a different part of the house will only create barrier frustration, and your dog, separated from the fun party, will become increasingly more rambunctious with time. Eventually, when other people come over, his anxiety will increase. Then he'll *really* become a nuisance. He could even become destructive.

Solution

Train your dog how to behave around guests. Invite guests over for a "dog training party." Serve cocktails and hors d'oeuvres, and explain that you're training your dog to be a well-mannered dog at parties. Your guests will have a blast reinforcing good behavior with you.

He can learn to "go say hello," or to offer a "sit" for a scratch on the head or a cookie. You can teach "go to your bed" by throwing a yummy treat onto his bed. Voice mark with "good" as he arrives at the bed and eats the treat. Soon you and your guests can tell him "go to your bed," and he'll do it gladly. Be creative, but don't lock him away.

Of course, if your dog is truly aggressive and would puncture or break the skin of another person or dog, you'll need professional help.

Create a dog who loves children

I'm sure you don't need a lawsuit. I get calls every year after the family dog bites the family child. Even the dogs you least suspect will discipline a child if pushed far enough. This is most important around the food bowl or bones, where most bites happen. It's hard to give an exact age, but I don't like leaving children under age seven or eight, depending on maturity level, alone with a dog.

People always call me *after* their dog has bitten their child or the neighbor's child. Don't wait to "see" if your dog likes children by letting him loose off the leash in the presence of kids, especially if your dog has never seen children before, or if you're not sure if he's seen them before. Prevention is key.

Solution

Create a dog who loves children. Start early. No puppy under four months can be dangerous under supervision around a child if done properly. Children under age seven really have to be supervised at all times. Make it easy for yourself if you have kids by designating an area for your dog, such as a run or a crate, where the kids aren't allowed to go unless you can be there. Dogs and young children *alone* usually don't mix.

Have all the children in the house practice hand feeding the dog for a few weeks. During this period, *all* the dog's food comes from the children. Also, try placing a cookie in the child's hand, and then voice mark (see Chapter 1) and treat the pup for taking the cookie from the child. Depending on child's age and maturity level, he may even be able to cue the dog to "sit." See if he can! You pup will learn to see the kids as food providers and controllers of valuable resources instead of seeing the kids as threats to his resources. Teach the children how to leave the dog alone if he walks away from them or if he's eating.

Arrange lots of play time, petting, and walks around children. Try taking your dog to a children's playground and sitting in a love circle. Have the puppy in the middle, and take turns feeding treats and petting the puppy. He should love this, and again, it's *supervised* to make sure both the pup and the children have a good experience. If the puppy starts to "play bite," simply pick him up and end the play. Or have him on leash and walk him away from all the food, kids, and excitement. He'll learn that every time he "puppy bites" someone's hands, the games and fun and food come to an end. Have kids represent "I'm getting a cookie" rather than "kids are a threat to my cookies." Change your dog's mind about what kids are and can be…the source of really good, yummy treats.

For an older dog, extreme care must be taken. Hire a professional trainer to screen the dog around children—preferably someone trained to read a dog's body language. Keep your dog on a leash and supervised at all times, and if he shows any negative sign (fearfulness, backing away, growling, staring), this could mean he's never seen a child and therefore could potentially be aggressive. Don't take any chances if you're not sure. If you have children and you are rescuing a dog, find out his history. Maybe it came from a family of five; this would be a good one for you. If the shelter is not sure, then don't put your children or someone else's children at risk.

GAME

GRAB MY TAIL/GRAB MY EARS

This game is great if you have children or not. No matter what, your kids *will* grab the dog's tail and ears, so you might as well teach him to *love* it.

Have a long piece of string cheese in your hand. As you *gently* pull the dog's tail, feed him a bite of the string of cheese at the exact same time.

Then, let go of the tail and stop feeding. Repeat. Grab the tail and feed at that exact time.

Now have your kids grab the tail as you feed, and then have everyone take their hands away. Repeat. Now have your child touch the dog's ear, while you feed cheese at the exact same time. Repeat.

Soon, the dog associates ear touching and tail pulling with wonderful rewards. Practice five to ten repetitions, three times a day, for a few weeks. Create a dog who *loves* having his tail grabbed and his ears pulled. If you don't train him to love it, he most certainly will tell the children that he does *not*. Try this fun game to prevent your dog from "snapping" the children away!

Puppies and babies

Being pregnant or having an infant will not allow you the proper time you need to train your dog. If you have a normal, friendly dog, there are several things you can do to prepare him for the addition of a baby into the home. If you truly have an aggressive dog and you're having a baby, you should probably think about finding a better home for your dog.

Solution

Prepare your dog for a baby. You can play tapes of a baby crying as your pup eats his dinner. He'll associate the baby's cry with getting fed, and the screams won't stress him out. Eventually, he'll learn to like the cry. Get a fake baby doll, and practice holding it and paying attention to it to see if your dog begins to nudge you or bark for attention. Some dogs don't mind at all, and others get very anxious. Have a bowl of treats ready, and as you're holding your fake baby, throw treats on a nearby dog bed and tell him to "go to your bed." Practice this every day.

When the real baby comes, just say, "Go to your bed," and he should know the behavior. In fact, holding your baby becomes an "environmental cue" for your dog to go lie down on his spot for a yummy bone. He'll look forward to you holding the baby, instead of competing and resorting to unwanted attention-seeking behaviors. You won't even have to tell him after a while—it will become automatic.

Consider hiring a dog walker during the first few weeks after the arrival of your baby. You don't want the dog to feel neglected because of the baby's presence. He will understand that all the attention is being given to the baby, so take extra care to still exercise and have some quality alone time with your dog. Your dog walker can help take some of this responsibility off your hands.

You can even let your dog eat out of your infant's hands. Of course, the baby can't really hold the food, but you can hold the baby's hand inside your hand, face up, and let the dog eat some treats out of the baby's palm. This way he'll see the baby as a food provider, not a threat to his food bowl, and he'll smell the baby's hand as he eats the food. As soon as children are old enough, they should begin hand feeding the dog for a few months. The dog will learn that his food comes from children's hands, and he'll be much less likely to show aggression toward them. Remember, a dog is always capable of biting—even the best, well-trained, and well-mannered dog can bite if pushed far enough beyond his limits. Every year, family dogs bite children in the family. This is extremely common, so be sure to properly socialize your baby, children, and dogs to help prevent a potential incident.

SOCIALIZATION TIPS

♦ **RELAX.** When you are nervous about meeting another dog, your dog will pick up on your nervous energy and follow suit. Your dog looks to you for cues on whether or not a new situation is good or bad. If you are nervous or unsure of yourself, the interaction between two dogs who are greeting could be stiff and strained. Slacken up your leash, bend down, and pet the other dog as you say hi in a friendly, happy voice. Now your puppy should relax, too.

♦ **START EARLY.** One of the biggest mistakes I see owners making is to begin the process of socialization too late. The socialization period lasts until about twenty weeks of age. That is when the pup is most impressionable and forms his ideas about the world, people, and other dogs. Ironically, this is the exact time that your pup is going through his vaccinations. Many people keep their dogs away from other dogs, walks, and the outdoors during this time. This will create a fearful and, most likely, an aggressive dog. This is the time your dog learns about his world. He needs to learn how to greet other dogs, people, and situations in this short time frame, or you'll need behavioral training later on. You should still be careful not to go to dog parks or "dirty" areas such as hikes where many wild animals have roamed the night before. Find clean neighbors' lawns and vaccinated, friendly dogs, and set up play dates.

♦ **MEET NEW PEOPLE.** Make sure your pup meets a lot of new people every day. Children, the elderly, people of all shapes, sizes, and colors. This is very important. If your pup doesn't see a variety of people, he could become fearful of them later. Fear almost always leads to aggression. Have other people feed your pup. Carry around a bag of treats, and every new person you meet can give him a yummy treat. Especially if your pup is fearful, use food. Having the stranger feed your pup changes his mind from "This person is frightening" to "I can't wait to take a cookie from people!"

♦ **TRAIN YOUR DOG.** There's nothing like training to enhance your dog's communication with you and the world around him. By creating a common language, you'll have a brighter, happier dog. If he acts fearful of a situation or person, give him something else to do, like "sit" or "come" for a treat. Then have other people give him commands as well.

♦ **KEEP IT POSITIVE.** Training and socializing have one very important thing in common: positive reinforcement. Be happy and have fun. If you are a drag, or fearful, or unsure, or too rough, your dog will not like his training or socializing. Use treats, and don't yell and scream at your dog. Realize that any mistake your dog makes is your fault, and you need to go back and retrain.

♦ **NEW EXPERIENCES.** Go on different walks. Go on hikes. Go to the snow. Teach him how to swim (see Chapter 9). Don't be boring and do the same thing every day. Create new and exciting adventures for a well-rounded pup.

♦ **MANNERS.** A well-socialized pup lives with good manners from the beginning. It's really cute when your eight-pound pup jumps up on you. When he becomes eighty pounds, now you have a huge problem. This is also not fair to the dog. Jumping was once "cute" and praised when he was young, but now that he's full grown you expect him to stop a behavior that you reinforced. Stop bad manners *early*. Prevent jumping by getting down and giving attention on the dog's level. He wants to be up near your face. Or give him something to do instead of jumping, like "sit" (if you've taught him this), which he knows is reinforced with treats and attention. If he still jumps, turn your back and leave the room immediately. When he realizes that jumping separates him from you, he'll stop. Don't pay attention to behaviors you do not want.

♦ **KNOW YOUR BREED.** You owe it to your dog to understand what he's made of. This will help you create training, exercise, and a lifestyle that's right for him. If you get a breed that's wrong for you, you will not be able to give your pup what he needs to have a well-rounded life. A sedentary person should not get a Jack Russell terrier. Period. It's just as important to know your "mix" of breeds. Maybe he was designed to chase prey and bark critters out of holes. Knowing this will help you be more tolerant and find creative ways and outlets for your dog to be himself. You can build a sandbox, for example, and teach your dog to dig in that instead of in the grass.

♦ **COMMITMENT.** Make sure you have the time to commit to getting a pup. If you don't have the time, don't even think about getting the dog. Really examine your own life, and make sure you are ready, or else you'll add to the list of bad owners who create aggressive, fearful dogs who eventually end up biting. Last year there were 4.7 million people bitten, and 800,000 of them sought medical care. Keep in mind, these are only the bites that were reported. Usually, bites come from a dog with little or no socialization.

♦ **A SURFACE A DAY.** When I have a pup, I make it a point to go on a different surface each day. This helps to teach them about the world. When greyhounds come off the track, they've spent their total time on a dirt track or a cement cage floor. When you rescue a greyhound, it's almost a given that you have to teach them how to walk on tile, grass, stairs, carpet, and many other floor surfaces. Believe it or not, these things scare the dog because he's never seen or experienced them, and he has no idea what they are. If your dog is older and fearful of a surface, use food and gently encourage your dog onto the new surface. Let him see you lying down on the surface. If he's small, you can pick him up and gently put him down near you on the new surface and begin to feed him yummy treats, pet him, and talk in happy tones. Puppies are willing, eager, and curious for new experiences. They'll walk onto new surfaces like cake. That's why it's important to do it early on.

♦ **NOISES.** I also try to let my pup experience noises. Trucks, motorcycles, cars, garbage trucks, fireworks, ball games, horns, whistles, screaming babies and children, pots and pans, kitchen timers, microwaves—you name it, we hear it. When you consciously train your new dog, you can at first make a very gentle noise. Maybe you hit a pot on the floor very quietly, just enough so that it doesn't scare your pup, and then treat him with a yummy snack. Gradually, you can get louder and louder with the noise, and he should still want to investigate, or at least not mind, the noise. Every time a loud noise happens in the environment, treat, play, and praise your dog. Take advantage of loud noises by wearing your treat pouch at all times with your pup or dog, and when a new or scary or loud noise occurs, immediately praise and treat your dog. For my Aussie's first 4th of July, we sat with a whole chicken and waited. Every time a firecracker went off, my pup got a piece of chicken. Pretty soon he was salivating when a firework went off. By the end of the night, he'd wag his body and come running to me for a treat. He's loved fireworks ever since.

Chapter 3

Reinforcement and Reward

What is reward?

A reward is something your dog *loves*. In the beginning, it's best to use primary reinforcement (food) as a reward. Praise—saying, "Good dog"—is *not* enough for your dog to learn a new behavior. You have to know what your dog absolutely loves. Here, I will list my dog's favorite rewards: chicken, steak, cheese, fish, milk bones, jerky treats, greenies, cow hoofs, bully sticks, raw marrow bones, a walk, a game of tug, a tennis ball, a rubber ball, another dog, a squirrel, and swimming. Yes, I even know the order in which he'd choose these things.

Your dog will *always* choose the most rewarding scenario. You need to figure out what your dog loves, and then you can begin to use these things as a reward for wanted behaviors. A reward is a consequence—a *good* consequence. Consequences drive behavior. Reward makes it possible for your dog to learn and repeat desired behaviors. Reward is not something *you* like—it's something your *dog* likes.

If listening to you always means that something *good* will happen (reward), then your dog will *choose* to listen to you. If listening to you means the end of fun in *any* way, your dog will never listen to you.

Solution

Create consistent, rewarded behaviors, and then teach your dog how to listen in the face of distractions. In the beginning, every behavior you ask for from your dog should have a reward. When your dog understands his basic commands and can even do them with distractions around, you can begin to reward intermittently. In fact, distractions can even become his greatest reward.

Rewarding with primary reinforcement

Primary reinforcement is something that is crucial to your dog's survival: food. Food can be an extremely pleasurable experience for both humans and dogs. Why not use it to teach your dog a new behavior? If you don't, you're stuck using force. Which would *you* rather have? Food? Or someone forcing you to do something?

Solution

Always have yummy treats around. Wear a pouch filled with yummy treats, and make training worthwhile and fun. Voice mark and treat all wanted and good behaviors. Dogs who have food rewards learn more quickly and retain the behavior for longer than dogs who are taught to behave using force, correction, or punishment.

Think about it: if training means that there may be a "correction" or "punishment" involved, then training is a risk. Your dog will eventually learn not to like training because of the chance of punishment. Instead, training should mean the opposite: the chance to earn delicious rewards! Use food and have fun. Eventually, you'll go to a schedule of intermittent reinforcement, and eventually he'll never know when the treat is coming. Keep it interesting and fun, and be consistent with the rewards in the beginning.

POSITIVE REINFORCEMENT

Positive reinforcement occurs when a behavior that is desired is rewarded with food, praise, and a toy—anything your dog sees as a reward for displaying a particular behavior. For example: the dog sits at your request, and you immediately pop a yummy treat into his mouth. When your dog comes when called, you throw the ball for him to chase (assuming he loves the ball more than anything). When your dog stops at the doorway, you "release" him through for a walk. Everything your dog loves can become a reward.

Understand reinforcement

If you constantly call your dog to come to you and there's nothing in it for him, he'll eventually stop coming to you. As I've explained before, consequences drive behavior. If someone told you to go to work today without pay, you wouldn't go. But if someone told you you'd get paid double, you may be there in double the speed. Your dog's behavior works the same way. Don't expect your dog to follow your cues or to "work" for you, unless you "pay him" with positive reinforcement. In the beginning, this means primary reinforcement: high-value food for a motivated dog.

Solution

Create a system of rewards. Every time your dog does something right, like "sit" or "come" or "shake a paw," add an immediate reward. Rewards can be food and praise, or toy and praise. But there must be something in it for him. It's ridiculous when I hear people say that they will not use treats to train. There must be a reward. He also must associate the reward with the behavior. Soon, the behavior itself becomes rewarding because you've paired it with something positive for so long.

For example, take Django, my Search and Rescue dog. In the beginning, he had tons of rewards for finding people. We started off doing extremely short problems, and gradually added more and more difficulty. Today, he is a fully certified, Mission Ready Search Dog, and he searches for the sheer pleasure of it. He gets so much joy out of the process that now the process alone is enough.

Great agility dogs are the same way. In the beginning, you use food and toys to teach new behaviors, and by the end of the process (which can take several months to years), the process of running agility is more rewarding than the reward itself. It's great to look at competitive or working dogs and see how obedient they are and how much joy they get out of being "obedient." In fact, I hate the word obedient. My dogs think "sit," "down," etc., are opportunities for praise and reward. They think obedience is a fun game. This is done with positive reinforcement.

Once the dog fully understands the behavior, you can move to a more intermittent reward schedule. Now that he knows the wanted behavior and loves to do it, he'll never know when the reward is coming. He may have to do twenty behaviors to get a reward, or maybe only one. This keeps it interesting and unpredictable.

Conversely, if I want to extinguish a behavior, I give no reward. If the rewards cease altogether, so will the behavior. Ignore a barking dog, and eventually he'll stop barking. Ignore a dog when you call him to come (by not rewarding), and eventually he'll stop coming. When people ask and wonder when they can *stop* rewarding, I say, "You can stop rewarding when you want the behavior to exist no longer!"

Using distraction as reward

People look at me cross-eyed when I say this, but it's true. If you use your dog's most powerful distraction as a reward, you'll have tremendous results. Yes, I really mean taking the *biggest* distraction for your dog and using it as a reward for wanted or asked for behaviors. For example, one of my client's dogs Burger is obsessed with squirrels. If there was a squirrel around, you could absolutely *never* get Burger's attention, much less get him to "come" away from the squirrel.

Here's what we did. First, beginning in the house where there were no distractions, we trained Burger to "come" by running madly away from him and having a treat ready when he "caught" us. When that behavior was learned, we brought Burger to the squirrel park. This is a fenced-in park with a *ton* of squirrels. We took Burger out of the car, and he was shaking with excitement. We had him on a leash. We had him hungry. He was just staring and shaking and looking at all the squirrels. We waited. Soon Burger realized he was on the leash, gave up on the squirrels, and came sniffing our treat pouches for some chicken.

At that *very* instant, we released Burger with an "okay" to go chase the squirrels. He did not, however get the chicken.

We then called Burger to "come" and began to move away, like we had in the living room at home. Burger came running madly *away* from the squirrels to get a bite of chicken. As soon as he took the chicken (his reward for coming to us), we immediately released him with an "okay" back into the squirrel kingdom. We let him chase, run, and bark at the squirrels and then called "come," and wouldn't you know it, we had Burger running *away* from squirrels, for chicken! He understood that "come" meant chicken *plus* squirrels, and he learned to double his reward. He thought, "Coming away from squirrels is fun! It does *not* mean the end of squirrels. In fact, it means that I get to sprint to you for a piece of chicken, and then I get to charge at the squirrels again! Doubling my pleasure!"

Distractions will *always* win out over you. You will *never* be as exciting as live prey to your dog unless you learn how to use the distractions to your advantage.

Let's take another example. When a dog learns that "come" means "come away from that other dog," he'll simply learn never to come to you because it means the end of potential play or greeting. To counter this, I begin by taking my dog outside on a leash and having a friend outside with his dog on the leash, too. I use one of my dog's favorite dogs for this game. I go outside with my dog on the leash and some yummy filet mignon. Instead of going right up to the other dog—which my dog wants more than *anything*—I say "come" and gently guide him to me using the leash (he will not come to you without one at this point). When he turns to "come" to you, feed him the steak, and then run madly with him toward the other dog. Let him sniff and play for a while, then back up to the end of your leash and call him to "come" again. He will usually choose to willingly come this time for a bite of meat. Then, you release him again into play.

He is now learning to "come" away from other dogs, and, if he does, he *always* gets to go back into play again. "Come" means the beginning of play *plus* a treat. It does not mean the end of play.

When it's time to end the session, rather than calling him to "come," simply go and get your dog, or else you risk poisoning the "come" command. After a few sessions, every time you see another dog, your dog will choose to look at you, so he can be "released" into greeting and play. Soon, you will not need the treats. Being "released" into play and greeting the other dog becomes the reward for "coming" to you. It's one of the best concepts you'll ever teach your dog, and the *only* way he'll ever choose you over distractions.

Now when you are in a situation where you *really* need to call your distracted dog, it will work. But there's one rule. For every *one* time you call your dog out of play and do *not* let him go back, you need to train *ten* rounds of "come" where you let him go back into the play. If you do not do this, you'll poison the "come" command, and your dog will never come to you if something is more exciting—and there will *always* be something more exciting.

Using freedom as a reward

If your puppy is free to run amok all the time, then freedom can't be used as a reward for wanted behaviors, such as going potty in the correct spot.

Solution

Use freedom as a reward. Regulate your pup's freedom, especially while you are training, so that freedom can be used as a valuable reward.

When potty training a pup, be sure to give him free time off leash as a direct reward for potty outside. As *soon* as he potties in the right spot, the leash comes off, and you have a play session in the backyard (as long as it's safe and fenced in). Soon, your dog will be pulling you toward the potty spot, because he knows that as soon as he potties there, he gets free time off leash.

A simpler version can be done before you open the back door to go out for a play session. Tell your dog to "sit" or "down." As a reward, the door opens, and you go out to have a play session.

Freedom can be an extremely powerful training tool for all commands when done correctly. Remember, you must be out playing with him for his freedom to be considered fun. Freedom is not fun if you're in the house and your pup is in the yard staring in at you.

Reward instead of bribe

Get the "visual" presence of food out of the learning picture as soon as possible.

Solution

Reward rather than bribe once your dog knows a behavior. For example, ask your dog to "sit," and when he does, you give him a cookie as a reward. If he does not sit and you reach into your pocket for a cookie to lure him into "sit," you've just bribed him. If you ask your dog to "sit" and he doesn't sit, leave the room. He's just lost his opportunity for a treat.

Reward removal

"Reward removal" is a very powerful tool. This occurs when your dog's opportunity to receive a reward is taken away. Parents use reward removal with their children all the time. Little Ben knows he gets ice cream if he finishes homework. If he does not finish, he does not get ice cream. This is a very powerful motivator.

The removal of the reward can be a great way to get faster, stronger behavior from your dog. Ask your dog to "sit" by luring him with a yummy snack. If he sits, give him the snack. If he doesn't sit immediately, walk away and try again in thirty seconds. See how fast you can get the "sit" to happen using this method of removing the potential reward. It's really fun. This can be applied to every command your dog knows. Stand near the front door, and call your dog to come. If he doesn't come to you, go on the walk without him. He just lost his chance to go on a walk. Take a thirty-second walk, come back, and try again. Do this every time you want to take your dog out.

As an exercise, think of how many ways you can use reward removal. Another great example is with jumping dogs. Have some cheese or cookies in your hand, and stand near a jumper. Be sure to be near a door where you can remove yourself and the yummy treats. If the dog jumps, run out the door without him. He just lost you, and the treat. Double whammy. Come back in. If he jumps again, remove yourself again. Don't say anything. Just leave. Keep playing until the dog doesn't jump. When he finally does not jump, give him the treat, and stay a while.

HUMAN IMPLICATION

At a Thanksgiving party, my friend was trying to get her one-year-old son to eat. She knew he was hungry, and she kept trying to shove the food at him.

I said, "Let me try." I held up the yogurt snack, said, "Yum," and offered it to the son. He shook his arms at me as if to tell me to go away. So I said, "Okay, then!" and I ate the treat myself. Then, I reached into the bag again, and offered him another one. He took it and shoved it into his mouth right away. It might have looked like magic, but I knew exactly what I had done. The second time I offered the snack, he knew he had to take it right away, or else I would eat it. You should have seen the speed at which he grabbed the snack out of my hand and shoved it into his mouth. It also made him feel like he was making a choice to eat it, and it made him laugh.

Motivate your dog

"Okay, ready? Good. Sit down because we are going to learn how to speak Hungarian today." Well, I'll tell you right now, unless a person is really motivated to learn a foreign language, it's probably not going to happen. Now, if I were to say to you, "Sit down. I'll give you one million dollars if you can learn to speak Hungarian," your motivation has changed.

Motivation. We've all felt it, and we all know what it means. Over and over again, I say to my clients that a dog needs to be *motivated* before you begin training. Basically, your dog needs the million-dollar jackpot in order to learn new behaviors. He won't listen to you if he doesn't find listening to be rewarding. Would you? When you train with an unmotivated dog, he'll be distracted, and no learning will take place. In fact, he'll learn precisely the opposite of what you want: he'll learn to *ignore* you. You and your voice become an annoyance. When something else is more exciting than you, your dog will not listen.

Solution

You need to be the most exciting thing for your dog. This can be trained and created by you and only you.

First, begin training in the house where you are the most exciting thing around. Don't try to train out in the real world. When your dog's behavior is 80% consistent, you may start to add distractions, but slowly. Just because you've trained in the living room does not mean your dog will "come" to you in the dog park, where there are hundreds of new and interesting distractions. Train your dog that *you* are the running, squeaking squirrel that he wants to pay attention to, and your dog will surely be willing to listen. Say your dog's name out of the blue. When he looks at you, toss a treat. Now you're creating a dog who is motivated to respond and look at you when you say his name.

Get your dog when he's hungry. Really hungry. Train before meals. Or better yet, train *for* a meal. Take the dry kibble, put it in a treat pouch, and train all day long. You can give him one kibble at a time (if you've got time) or call him to "come," and feed him his whole meal out of your hands. As I explained in the first chapter, hand feeding is a great tool. Hand feed for a few weeks, and then ask your dog for behaviors so he can "earn" his food. If that's the way he eats, he really should look forward to "coming" and "sitting" for you.

If your dog loves a ball or a tug toy, this should be incorporated into training as well. Remember, anything your dog loves can become a reward for desired behavior. If your dog loves the tennis ball, make him "sit" before you throw the ball. If your dog loves his walk, make him stop first at the front door. You are using the walk as the reward for stopping at the front door. Again, this will only be valuable if he loves the reward you have to offer him. If you don't know what motivates your dog, try a twenty-four-hour fast. I guarantee you, the pickiest eater will become incredibly motivated by food if he doesn't have it for a while. In no way am I suggesting you starve your dog. Twenty-four hours is nothing for a fully-grown, healthy dog to go without food. He's not a baby. In the wild, dogs may go two weeks without eating. Just make sure he has plenty of water.

Uncomfortable with the "no food" approach? Then feed dry kibble only for meals, and get something incredibly smelly and yummy for training, like chicken, steak, cheese, or liver snacks. Don't train unless your dog is motivated. If he's "kind of" motivated, he'll be "kind of" trained.

Choosing to listen vs. having to listen

Dogs can learn a new behavior by reward (food or toy paired with praise), or they can learn to do something by avoiding correction. The latter is a sad situation, which creates a fearful dog. For example, I've seen people physically push their dog's butt down to teach him to sit. They say, "Sit," and if he doesn't sit, they mush his butt to the floor. Not only can this hurt your dog's legs, he'll only learn to sit because he doesn't want to be pushed into the floor. Ouch. I'd rather have a dog who sits because he loves to sit, not because he has to sit.

Dogs who are physically manipulated or yanked into a position show stress and anxiety. When this "forced" dog is finally off a leash somewhere, he is destined not to listen because he knows he can get away from you. This creates that "sneaky" behavior—as soon as you unhook the leash, your dog will disobey and won't listen to you. I wouldn't listen to you either.

Children rebel in a negative environment the same way. When a parent is too domineering, the child wants to get away. Try forcing a child to do something. It will never work. He might "behave" in the presence of the parents, but he's sure to act out in other areas, and he certainly won't behave when you aren't around.

If you create a good reward system, eventually your dog will behave and listen because he associates it with fun. He will be *motivated*. My dogs love to "sit" and "come"—they're happy to do it. I bring out the treats every once in a while, and it keeps it exciting.

Spoil your dog for the right reasons

Have you ever seen the dog who has everything, but he's fat, lazy, and unhappy? Like a child who has everything, he becomes spoiled and unmotivated. If you "feel sorry" for your dog and give him two hundred toys and treats all day long, he'll have nothing to look forward to or be motivated by.

Solution

Rotate toys, control food and treat intake, and train when your dog is hungry. If your pup always has everything he wants, then he probably feels the way you feel on Thanksgiving Day: full. Yuck. A full dog wants to sleep and won't be motivated for training, or even to take a walk or a hike. He can even become obese and diabetic.

Your dog's motivation level is also affected by breed and age, so don't expect a thirteen-year-old Akita to be super excited about training. Nothing against Akitas, but be realistic about goals, and take age and breed into account.

You create your dog's motivation. The best way to do this is to teach your dog that he always has a *chance* at winning a big jackpot.

GAMBLING AND JACKPOTS

Casinos sure understand how to train people. They have figured out the power of intermittent reinforcement and jackpots. This keeps people coming back, and even causes some people to form an addiction to gambling. Casinos are based on this schedule of reinforcement: unpredictable, random, and intermittent, with a possibility of a JACKPOT.

To apply this, first you reward your dog for every correct behavior. "Sit" gets a treat every time, until the behavior is about 80% reliable, even with distractions. Once you've achieved this, you can begin a random schedule of reinforcement. Really keep it varied. Sometimes give a treat for every five behaviors cued; sometimes give a treat every single time. One day, give no treats for cued behavior, and the next day, give a jackpot for just one "sit." A jackpot is a flooding of treats, maybe ten or even twenty small bites in a row! This will really keep your dog performing, listening, and loving it, especially with the chance of a jackpot. Try to get a behavior 80% reliable, then move to a random reward and jackpot system. This always keeps it interesting for the pup!

Be aware of what you are rewarding

This seems simple, but it's really very subtle. It's hard to see what behaviors you're actually reinforcing with your pup.

Solution

Think about it. In the beginning, you really must take the time to stop and think, "Okay, am I rewarding this bad behavior in some way?" Really take a long, hard look at how your dog behaves…it's usually always a reflection of you. I know it's hard to hear, but this is almost always the case. When you become aware of what is driving your pup's behaviors, you can start to work on the problems correctly instead of accidentally rewarding unwanted behaviors.

Train an alternative behavior

Just the other day, I saw a woman at a coffee shop with a very rambunctious, exuberant cattle dog. The pup was about four months old and was biting people's ankles as they walked by. When he couldn't reach someone's ankle, he'd get frustrated and turn his instinct on his owner, transferring the excitement in a mad, passionate fit of biting her hands and pant legs. I call it "killing it" when they shake their heads back and forth. You see, by biting and chasing the ankles, the person keeps walking on. That alone reinforced the dog. By chasing people, they move away like sheep.

Solution

Teach an alternative behavior. If your dog likes biting ankles, give him something just as exciting instead, like a tug toy. When you see someone walking by, and you notice your herding dog focusing on his herding instinct, begin to squeak your tug toy and run alongside your dog until he bites onto his toy. Give him an alternative outlet for his herding instinct. Now when he sees ankles, it could mean a game of tug with you, instead of "killing" someone's pant leg.

There's nothing wrong with distracting the dog with a treat or toy, but timing is everything. The treat or toy can come for "sitting," not biting ankles. Think about what behavior you are rewarding all the time, and practice rewarding alternative behaviors, such as "sit" or "speak," rather than reinforcing unwanted behaviors.

HUMAN IMPLICATION

Watch out for rewarding negative or undesired behaviors. When my ex-husband used to get in "moods," I would constantly try to make it better. As a result, I would actually reinforce his bad mood by paying copious amounts of attention to him. I'd say, "What's wrong, honey?" Or, "Can I get you anything?" This is precisely what he wanted. His mood would always perpetuate because it got him so much attention. By the way, his mother did this with him when he was a child.

One day, I decided to ignore the mood completely. I didn't play an "ignoring" game; I simply went about my business, leaving him alone. Within minutes of my not paying attention to his mood, he got up, came into the bedroom, and asked me how my day was. It was mind blowing.

Association

Dogs learn by association. And consequence. Every single thing your dog does has a specific association or consequence for him: a noise, a certain person enters the room, a car ride—everything. For example, every time you pick up the leash, a walk happens. Pretty soon, the leash alone causes the dog to become happy and excited. Go ahead, pick up a leash and watch your dog get excited. Now imagine everything in your dog's world is that powerful. You have the ability to create a dog who associates people with good things or bad things. Do car rides bring us to the vet? Or to the dog park? If the car only brings the dog to boarding facilities and vets, naturally he will hate the car.

If the car brings the pup to fun and exciting and new places, he'll love the car, and the few times it takes him to the vet will not matter as long as you've spent most of the time going to fun places.

Everything has an association or a consequence. My favorite story involves Ritz Cracker, the golden retriever who was the mouthiest dog in the world. He did nothing but put your entire arm in his mouth, all the time. The family had three kids who reinforced this behavior by screaming, squeaking, and running like mad when Ritz put his mouth on their arms or legs. Ritz was just playing, but the mouthing caused the kids to run like real live prey, and Ritz could then chase them and mouth again. Ritz had invented his own game. I simply put a leash on Ritz, and we made a new and improved game. Ritz loved to be inside with the family and kids. With this new game, every time Ritz put his mouth on anyone at all, we'd pretend this meant that he wanted to go outside. As soon as Ritz put his mouth on you, you had to grab the leash, put him outside, and separate him from the family. Then we'd let him back in, and he'd mouth again. Immediately we'd rush him out and leave him by himself, which he did not like. Ritz mouthed only four times before he understood it had a new consequence: "When I used to mouth, kids would squeal and run and I'd chase; now when I mouth, I get separated from my family. I think I'll stop mouthing." We taught Ritz to fetch a ball and a stuffed rabbit, which was much better to mouth anyway.

My next favorite story, and a very important one, was teaching Dug's owners to play dead. Yes, I taught the owners to play dead, not the dog. Dug is some kind of wheaten terrier mix, and he has this really bad jumping-up-and-biting-and-nipping behavior. He jumps on and bites his owners in an attempt to herd them, and he gets tremendous attention for this. For example, the owner Ron will be doing his own thing, like putting on his shoes. Dug will start this crazy behavior, almost attacking Ron with jumps, growls, and nips. Dug is actually playing and herding, and I asked Ron what was happening when Dug behaved this way. Ron explained that he's tried "everything" to control Dug. I explained that "everything" he actually did *had* to be reinforcing the dog, so I directed him to do the exact opposite. He had been reacting by trying to get the dog to "sit" or "stay" or "down," and these attempts were all actually reinforcing Dug's crazy behavior. Ron was doing his own thing, like putting on shoes, and Dug's behavior caused Ron to stop and "deal" with him. Instead, I told Ron to "play dead." Every time Dug acted crazy, Ron was to drop to the floor and die. No movement, no laughing. Again, instead of Ron becoming animated and dealing with Dug, Ron died. Dug learned very quickly that his crazy behavior was no longer reinforced, and it diminished 90%. We also gave him an outlet to be crazy. Tugging his toy when we said "get it" was a new game. If he tugged or tried to steal the toy without the "get it" command, then we'd play dead. This really worked wonders on Dug.

Change fear into curiosity with treats

A question I get all the time is, "Aren't you rewarding the dog's fear by adding a treat?" The answer is no. You are not rewarding a specific fear by treating your dog; you are actually changing his association with the fearful stimulus. Rewarding the fear would be to separate the dog from what he's afraid of. For example, the removal of a frightening person, noise, or object rewards his fear behavior; he thinks his fear made the object go away. Instead, we do the opposite, by adding a treat and changing his association.

Solution

Understand how treating affects your dog's associations. This will help you help your dog overcome a fearful situation.

CASE STUDY

Do treats reward a specific fear, or do they change the dog's association with the feared object or situation?

What follows is one of my favorite cases. It will show you how reward, food, and treats do *not* reward a dog's fear but can instead change his associations.

Let's take a wheaten terrier named Pickle. The owners called me in a hopeless state. Pickle was four years old and had never gone up the stairs in the house. The family didn't mind because they didn't want hair in the upstairs bedrooms anyway. So whenever the owners went upstairs, Pickle would just wait at the base of the stairs for them to come down.

Now, about six months earlier, Pickle had stopped going through the dog door. There were steps leading up to the dog door. Eventually, Pickle became afraid of all stairs, and the family couldn't take him to the beach because of the steps leading down. More and more, they had to leave Pickle at home for fear that they'd run into a staircase, and Pickle would wig out. Pickle had other fears, too, I learned, such as a fear of shadows coming through the window in late afternoon.

When I came over, we began with "go touch" for filet mignon. The dog immediately loved to target my palm. We taught Pickle that the palm of the hand meant "touch" by rubbing some steak on our empty palms. Of course, Pickle wanted to sniff the palm, and when he did, we gave him an actual piece of steak. We did about twenty rounds of this "touch" palm game and then gave him a break.

Next, we went to the base of the stairs in the house. I had the entire family go up the stairs and sit at the top with steak in their hands. I got on the first step, offered my palm, and said "touch." Pickle cautiously stepped onto the first step to take the meat. The family couldn't believe it. Note where I placed the family—at the top of the steps. We repeated this about five times, and gave Pickle another break. Breaks are very important, especially in high stress work.

Next we did the halfway game. I picked up Pickle, carried him exactly halfway up the stairs, and placed his front two feet on the lower steps, toward the base of the stairs, and his two rear feet back up the stairs so that he was pointing down the staircase. It's very important with the halfway game to calm the dog. I began feeding Pickle steak as I set him down in the halfway position, and he stood there eating filet for a while. Next, I let him follow me down to the base of the stairs. No steak for this part. Only steak for being on the stairs, halfway.

Next, I went up the stairs halfway and asked Pickle to "touch" my palm. This was a too far for him to feel comfortable, so I came down a little, three steps up, and he came up three steps to take the steak. Very successful for training session number one.

Now for the dog door. The family told me that they usually just let him in through the sliding glass door. What they didn't realize was that *that* was Pickle's reward for showing fear toward the dog door. The fear was reinforced by *not* having to deal with the dog door.

I told the family to leave him outside and never to let him in through the sliding human door. We put steak on the floor inside the dog door. He was frustrated, and started to bark and carry on. With Pickle, it was possible for me to pick him up and put him halfway through the dog door. Some dogs would not do well with that, but Pickle was small enough. If the dog is too large, do not do the halfway game. I put Pickle in halfway, and he did the second half by himself, eating the yummy steak on the other side. My instruction to the owners was to do the same games when I wasn't there, but also just to leave Pickle outside. When he's hungry enough, he'll come in.

The next time we took Pickle for a walk, we left through the front door. He loved his walk. However, in the backyard, there were six steps down leading out a back gate to the street. Perfect! I placed the family outside the gate. You could see that Pickle really wanted to go on his walk, but he had to go down the outside steps in order to do so. He did not come down the steps on his own, so we left on the walk *without* Pickle. He just learned that he missed his walk.

When we got back from the walk, Pickle had come down the steps on his own. We immediately grabbed his leash and took him for a short walk, and then came *in* through the back gate as well. He ran right up the steps, and it was almost unbelievable. We went back down the steps, and he did not want to come, so we did the halfway game. I placed Pickle halfway down the steps and instructed the family to go out the gate. Pickle remembered that we'd leave without him, and he immediately ran down the steps and got another walk.

I told them to work this way for a few weeks. Either they could leave without Pickle (on a walk) and Pickle would learn by not receiving his walk, or they could do the halfway game. All walks were to be taken this way. *No* leaving through the front door—only through the back gate, down the steps.

Next, we went into the house and waited for the 4:00 p.m. shadows. I didn't need to see the fear—that would be practicing his old behavior of fear, and we wanted to minimize and do away with *all* practicing of old, unwanted behaviors. We planned to have his favorite thing, a pig's ear, ready to go. Before the shadows came, we sat in the exact spot with the pig's ear and Pickle by our side. Eventually, with the change of light, the shadows came. Pickle backed up and began to spook at the waving shadows on the carpet. We sat on the shadows with the pig's ear and told Pickle to "touch." He willingly came to us and began to eat his chew on the rug. He was on a leash, which prevented him from taking the toy and running away. He ate his entire chew with the shadows on top of him. I instructed them to do this every day.

It was time to leave the first session, and Pickle's mom wanted to know how long I expected this rehabilitation to take. I said, "It depends on how motivated you are to do the work." I explained that it always depends on how consistent you are, and it depends on you not letting him practice his old ways, like coming through the sliding door instead of the dog door. It could take a few weeks to a few months because Pickle has been practicing this for four years, and he's not going to change over night.

Incredibly enough, I got a call the next day. It was Pickle's mom, saying that Pickle had just come through the dog door on his own! They had left him outside and went into the living room to watch TV. Suddenly, Pickle appeared. His old ways would not work anymore. The next week he went up the stairs willingly by himself. Did the treats and food increase and reward his fear? No, the treats and the food changed Pickle's association from one of fear to one of excitement. "I love the stairs," Pickle would say now, if he could talk. "Stairs give me steak, or they get me to go on a walk! Stairs are *good*. Stairs won't eat me, in fact, I eat on the stairs."

The family followed my instruction of leaving a food bowl with a little cheese, peanut butter, and chicken at the top of the stairs. Within a week, Pickle would bound up the stairs to see what new thing was in the bowl. And, for the shadows, they continue to give him a distracting bone instead of letting him bark at the shadows. He has learned to take his bone into the other room, and by the time he finishes the shadows are gone. Magic, he thinks; by eating this yummy bone, the shadows go away. Remember, before he thought that barking and cowering at the shadows made them go away. Pickle learned an alternative behavior. Chewing a bone makes the shadows go away. How easy.

Note: *Before doing exercises like these, be sure to rule out any medical issues your dog may have. For example, if Pickle had a hip or leg problem, he may have been scared of the stairs because they caused him pain. Make sure the cause of soiling the house, for example, isn't a bladder infection. Bladder infections cause a dog or a puppy to have uncontrollable urination very frequently. This is a medical problem, not a training problem. Always rule out any possible medical issues.*

Fear vs. anxiety

There is an important difference between fear and anxiety. Fear is healthy and normal. Without fear we'd all be dead. If a man comes toward me in an alley with a knife, I will run away. My fear causes me to have a flight response. If you're walking your dog and a really loud bang goes off (maybe it's the 4th of July), your dog has every right to be scared at that moment. Fear is a normal and healthy reaction to impending danger.

Sometimes, dogs will show fear when there is no real danger, but when they are only anticipating danger. This is called anxiety. Anxiety is living in a state of fear, thinking that something bad may happen at any time, even when there is no real threat. A constant state of anxiety isn't healthy for a dog, or a person.

Solution

Recognize fear, and prevent your dog from developing anxiety. All dogs and people will feel fear at certain points in their lives. If you know how to respond when your dog experiences fear, you can manage the fear and not allow it to progress into anxiety.

For example, the first time your dog sees a person dressed as a clown, he may bark. Some dogs even bark and show fear at people with large backpacks or bags, or people in uniform. What you do with your dog the very first time he encounters a frightening situation can really make or break your dog. But don't worry, even if your dog has generalized his fear into constant anxiety, there are things you can do to help.

Let's take Buggy, a dog I trained recently. Buggy was ten months old on his first Halloween. The family had kids, and everyone was donning their costumes. Buggy had been a normal dog until this night. On Halloween, the younger son came down the staircase toward Buggy in a ghost costume. Buggy began to bark, growl, and back up. The mother yelled at Buggy for growling and barking, and she threw him outside. Outside, Buggy continued to see people coming to the door and going into the house in crazy costumes, and he hid in the bushes and continued to bark.

Let's look at what happened. First of all, *poor Buggy*. He was simply scared of the ghost costume. At the moment he saw the costume he experienced fear, and then he was actually disciplined for showing that fear. At this point, the ghost costume became *really* frightening to Buggy because now it also meant that mom yelled at him and made him go outside. The scolding formed a very powerful association for Buggy. What it told him is that he should be even more scared of people in costumes because costumes also meant being scolded and thrown outside. He also learned that by growling and barking, the scary person went away. Buggy got away from the perceived threat by showing fear, and his fear was reinforced in that very moment. It's really very simple.

After Halloween, Buggy began to show fear of people in hats or long coats. His fear began to generalize. That's when the family called me. Without treatment, Buggy could have become "dogoraphobic." His fear could have begun to generalize to all people.

First, let's talk about prevention. As soon as you get your dog, young or old, begin to teach him to "go touch" safe objects. This is done simply by having your pouch full of yummy treats and going into the kitchen or living room. Keep in mind, you should do this exercise whether or not the fear has started. The key is to teach the dog to "go touch" objects or people that he is not in any way afraid of. The great thing about this game is that dogs will sniff any new object you hang down at nose level. So, take a fork, for example. When he sniffs the fork, voice mark the moment by saying, "Good," or "Yes," and immediately follow with a yummy treat. Next, take a candle, a book—really, any item in your house—and tell him "go touch." Again, when he puts his nose to the object, say, "Yes," and follow with a treat. Why are we doing this? So that eventually, we have a language to tell our dogs that it's okay to go touch and investigate potentially frightening things. If you prep your dog correctly, the first time he shows fear or "spooks" at something, you've created a powerful alternative behavior for your dog. Instead of showing fear and having that fear be reinforced, he can "go touch." When you are using your performance/task brain, you aren't using your fear brain. They are literally different parts of the brain. When you're doing a task, like math, for example, you can't be afraid. If you are, you won't be able to complete the math problem. By giving your dog another option, he will choose to "go touch" the object or person he's afraid of.

Buggy had already generalized his fear to people, hats, coats, and even glasses. I came over, and we began to teach Buggy to "go touch." The family worked on "go touch" by feeding Buggy all his meals this way. He simply loved to "go touch." The family was instructed by me only to touch things that were *not* scary to Buggy.

Two weeks later, I came back with hats, glasses, Halloween masks, and an assistant Buggy had never seen before. It was amazing. First, I rang the doorbell with a hat and glasses on. They answered the door, prepared with treats, and Buggy started to bark at me, growl, and back up. Immediately, the family walked forward toward me, and said, "Buggy, go touch!" At that moment, you could actually see the light bulb going off in Buggy's brain. He had a perplexed look on his face, like, "Really? If I touch this scary thing I'll get a liver treat?" And at that very instant, he stopped barking, came forward, and sniffed me. The family cheered, "Yes!" and immediately followed with a treat. Buggy was then wagging his tail and excited to see me, even in my hat and glasses. He had immediately changed his association from one of fear to, "People in hats and glasses are good, they have liver treats, and I can go touch them." When Buggy was in working/doing brain, he could not be in fear brain. It's physically impossible.

Next, I told my assistant to come to the door. She had on a hat, mask, and sheet as a robe. She rang the doorbell, and as soon as Buggy saw her, again he began to bark and back up. The family said, "Buggy, go touch!" and he immediately came over to investigate. Again, he got a "yes" and a liver treat. Buggy was learning: scary people are good, and scary people have liver treats. When this is taught over and over again, pretty soon scary people are not scary anymore. Buggy had changed his association. Don't wait until your dog is fearful to teach this command. Try to have it ready to go so that you know what to do the first time your dog shows fear. Without this helpful tool, fear could generalize, and your dog could experience the world living from one fearful moment to the next in a state of anxiety.

Counter-conditioning and desensitization

My Australian shepherd had a birthday party with other dogs and people when he turned one year old. I got a giant dog piñata and stuffed it with milk bones and dog treats. We used two fitted PVC pipes to make a long swing stick. All of a sudden, my friend Sarah was swinging blindfolded like a wild maniac. She hit the dog piñata, and with an extremely loud *crack*, the piñata exploded and the PVC pipe came apart, smashing my dog in the head. He ran off madly to hide. Because of that, in one split second, he developed a huge fear of loud noises.

Before that moment, my dog actually loved loud crashes and noises because I had desensitized him to noise. Once, we even had training at a firing range. But now, even the normal trash can at home, which had a metal lid that he'd heard a million times, began to terrify him. He would shake, go out the dog door, and hide in the yard.

Solution

Conquer fear through reward. That very same night, I began to counter-condition and desensitize my dog. Instead of following instinct, which says to go outside, pet, coddle, and cuddle the dog, my training mind got to work. I already had trained him the "touch" command. So I decided to make him touch objects that made a noise. For example, I'd drop a pan, and then I'd get really happy and say, "Go touch!" and he'd run over to investigate, touching his nose to the pan. I would then voice mark and treat. Suddenly, it became a fun game.

I began with a subtle noise, not too loud, and when he was consistently touching the source with no fear, I'd make a louder noise. I slowly worked up to louder and louder noises, and closer and closer to my dog. This whole process is known as counter-conditioning and desensitization. You are taking something the dog views as scary and negative and pairing it with something positive, until the dog changes his association from one of being scared to one of pleasure. We do this by pairing the loud noise with some really yummy treats. Soon, scary loud noises mean yummy treats! Within a few days, my dog was running toward loud noises, not running away.

Instead of chasing after your dog when he's fearful, walk away. Praise him when he decides to come out of hiding. If you always run after and follow your dog, his "hiding" behavior and fear is reinforced because it brings you to him.

Conquering fear through reward helps a fearful dog build confidence because the dog feels like he's in control of what's going to happen (the opposite of making him feel "submissive" or "weak"). When the dog is rewarded and successful at getting what he wants, he feels a sense of control over the environment. With this ability to control comes confidence, and fear diminishes. Help your dog deal with his fears before they generalize or turn into phobias.

Consistency

Inconsistency in training creates an inconsistent dog. Inconsistency can happen in a family of twenty or between a sole owner and his dog. In the beginning, too many different people training your pup can be confusing. Everyone sounds different and has slightly different ways of doing what appears to be the same thing.

Solution

Get the whole family on the same page, especially when the dog is first learning. Follow through, win, and be consistent every single day with your voice marking, timing, and reward vs. no reward.

Don't train when you know you can't follow through. If you call your pup to "come," he should be on a leash so that if he doesn't come, you can gently guide him toward you and reward when he gets to you. Do not train just to see if your puppy will come for no reward. Remember, withholding a reward is how we get *rid* of a behavior. For example, if you're on a phone call and you tell your dog to "down" and "stay," what are you going to do if he gets up? You're on the phone, and you have no way of being consistent or following through. Down the road, once he's trained he can listen to you when you're on the phone, but if you begin "kind of" training this way, you'll have a "kind of" obedient dog.

Everyone dealing with the dog has to be on the same page. Everyone must understand your voice markers, reward system, hand signals, what to do if your dog does not listen, and the use of timing and "no reward" as a consequence. Be consistent.

Chapter  4

A Physically Healthy Pet

Learning your dog's body

I've met owners who never touch or examine their dogs. I know this sounds weird, but it does happen. I have a client who had to have her dog put under anesthesia to pull a foxtail out of his foot. It had abscessed and become infected. My dogs would have just let me pull it out because I examine and check their paws and body almost every other day. Another client once called me about her dog's bad breath. I did recommend the vet, but when I got to the house, I instinctively just looked in the dog's mouth. There, stuck across the roof of his mouth, lodged between his upper teeth…was a rotting chicken bone. I picked it out, and boy, was it gross.

Being familiar with your dog can really help prevent moments like this. Some dogs don't allow their owners to look inside their mouths, turn them over, clip nails, etc. This can be dangerous. If you never examine your dog, and then eventually try to do so, his reaction may be to bite you. You need to pet, massage, feel, and be familiar with all parts of your dog: feet, ears, tail, toenails, eyes, face—all of him. This is important. He could have a tick on him, a hot spot, or a cut that's infected. He can't tell you if something hurts or feels uncomfortable, so you must examine him once in a while. If he won't "let" you, you need to work slowly until you can. This can be more like a game—it should never be forced. It's about creating a willing partner who lets you feel and examine his feet, mouth, ears, and entire body.

Solution

Examine your pup at least once a week. You want to learn to become familiar with every part of your dog when he's healthy, so that when something is wrong, you're more likely to notice.

Know what your pup's gums look like when they're healthy. Some gums are pink, and some are purple or even black-ish. If you know what color his healthy gums are, then you also can tell when something may be wrong. For example, light pink gums may turn very bright and dark pink when the dog is overheated. The tongue may also be very long and swollen with an overheated dog. Extremely pale gums may signify anemia. Yellow gums could mean jaundice and liver problems. However, some dogs have naturally pale-pink gums, and that's why it's important to note what color your dog is when he's healthy. Look at the ear color as well. You can do this every day. Gently look inside your dog's ear when he's healthy and especially when you notice lethargy or any change in your dog. Bring your dog to a vet right away at any detectable change in gum or ear color.

You should be able to feel your dog's teeth, gums, ears, toes, and feet. He should allow you to gently roll him over onto his side. Note: this is not a "flip" over. It's a very gentle roll. The dog must be extremely willing for this part of the exercise to take place. If any of this is difficult for you and your dog, you need to go slowly. Try feeding him a piece of cheese with one hand as you touch his feet with the other. If he still will not let you, continue hand feeding and bonding for a few more weeks, get him nice and tired, and try again. You can also have a partner help you. Have them feed the dog cheese, hot dog, or some soft food as you examine the feet, pretend you are "clipping" the nails, look inside the ears, and see and feel the teeth and gums. When paired with food, this usually becomes a very pleasurable exercise for the dog. My dogs actually come and "ask" me for this body massage. That's really what you are doing. Massage every part of your dog's body. Really rub those muscles, very gently at first, and with time, you can work into a real massage.

I recommend getting down onto the ground and putting your dog's back to you. Sit down behind your pup, and gently start scratching his chest. This exercise should always begin the same way to create predictability. Try really massaging and rubbing the chest until your dog relaxes, and then just let him go. Each time you do this, add another step. The next time, massage his chest, feel the mouth and gums, and then let him go. Try to let him go before he struggles away from you. Just think, wouldn't it be nice to know when you were getting an examination? If you always do it in the same position, it creates a language with your dog. He'll understand that it's examination time.

Begin slowly, and don't let your dog "tell" you he doesn't want you to examine him. He'll tell you by struggling, wiggling, growling, or even mouthing or biting you in extreme cases. Behaviors like this in a puppy don't necessarily signal aggression, but if you let him go when he struggles and bites at you, you're teaching him that his bite is powerful. Once your dog finds out he can intimidate you with his growl and teeth, you're doomed. The key is to begin slowly, use food, and make sure your dog is enjoying himself. When he willingly accepts your touch and exam, let him go. If he's struggling to get away from you, try later when he's tired and hungrier. Do not force him to do this exercise. You want to create gentle cooperation. He should love this, and it's great for bonding. Respect the dog, and he'll respect you.

Know a healthy dog

It's important to know what a healthy dog looks like and also to be able to recognize signs of illness. A healthy dog has bright, shiny eyes, a shiny coat, good appetite, is able to maintain an ideal body weight, and is playful and interested in you and his environment.

Signs of illness include lack of appetite, decrease in activity, weakness or lethargy, lack of interest in his environment or you, any loss of balance or coordination, weight loss, increased water consumption (which can be a symptom of kidney disease or diabetes), not grooming themselves, not drinking enough water, having a dull, lack-luster coat, or bad breath.

If you notice any of the signs of illness, see your vet immediately. Dogs should have periodic visits to the vet for routine check-ups. Prevention is the best cure. Make sure your pup always has a healthy, quality diet, training, exercise, attention, and time with you.

Brushing teeth

Dogs can get gingivitis and tooth decay just like humans. Most dogs don't like their teeth to be brushed, but this can be one of the best preventative measures you can take.

Solution

Brush your pup's teeth. If you start with a puppy, use your finger and begin by gently messaging the upper and lower gum line in a circular motion. This will not clean the teeth, but it will get your pup used to the motion. Also, invest in some turkey- or chicken-flavored dog toothpaste, put a little on your finger, and start brushing. Usually, the puppy loves it. Do the same thing with an older dog. It may take a little longer, but keep working with yummy toothpaste on your finger.

Eventually, after four or five finger-brushing sessions, I recommend the finger toothbrush that you attach right on the tip of your finger. Now, put the toothpaste on the finger brush, and brush away! If plaque is extremely bad, you may have to go in for a professional cleaning. But, if you've practiced correctly, they may be able to clean your dog's teeth without anesthesia because he's used to his mouth being examined and brushed.

Want a hug? How 'bout a stiff pat on the head?

Dogs do not like to be hugged. Please do not hug your dog or let other people hug your dog. Unless you are extremely familiar with a specific dog, you should never hug one.

Also, don't pat or slap your dog really hard. He would much rather be stroked gently. I know it sounds obvious, but I see this all the time. People pat their dogs extremely hard, and you can just see the dog recoiling. Be gentle. Dogs love gentle scratching and stroking, just like you.

Understand what your body signals to your dog

When you are unsure of yourself or are scared, you exhibit different body language than when you're feeling confident and happy. Your dog absolutely can pick up on your subtle body cues. In fact, he can even *smell* your slight change in perspiration levels, adrenalin, and excitement, and he can most likely smell your mood as well.

When you are nervous, your dog will get worried. This is why it's important to be a strong, confident partner for your dog. Your dog, like a child, looks to you for cues on what to do and how to act. People respond to body language the same way. You can see when a person is insecure or confident simply by their body language, so why wouldn't your dog?

Body language is how dogs communicate. In fact, studies have shown that most of the time, our "conversations" with people mean less than what our body is actually saying. We actually communicate through subtextual and nonverbal cues (subtle body language, facial expressions, and tone of voice). I could say, "Good morning," and mean, "I want to go out with you." Or I could say, "Good morning," and mean, "I'm not interested in you in the *slightest*," or, "Why are you waking me up this early?" You get the picture. Don't underestimate what your body and voice communicate to your dog.

If your voice sounds nervous or anxious when you meet other dogs, you are helping to create a tense greeting, which could turn into an altercation. This is your fault, not your dog's fault. I've seen perfectly healthy, normal dogs become aggressive simply because of their owners' fear and insecurity. Have people watch you working and training your dog, and ask them what they observed. Were you confident? Wimpy? Asking or begging instead of commanding confidently? All of this matters when creating a relationship with a dog, or a human.

PETTING MYTH—FEAR AND AGGRESSION

One of the biggest myths in dog training is that you shouldn't pet a fearful or aggressive dog because you will reinforce the fear or aggression. This is not at all true. Petting can soothe your dog and, as scientific research proves, it actually calms the nervous system.

Loose leash, please...slack it up!

The leash is your phone line to your dog. When people get nervous while walking their dog, they tend to tighten up on the leash, basically strangling their dog. This does several things. It signals to your dog that you are nervous, and he begins to associate other dogs or people with you being nervous. This will most certainly make him nervous and worried and could lead to aggressive interactions.

A tight leash also prevents your dog from being able to signal proper body language to the dog he's meeting. This causes the dog he is meeting to wonder why your dog isn't acting normal. Your dog will appear stiff or nervous to the other dog, which can make the other dog also feel nervous and threatened. This increases the chance of an altercation.

A tight leash is also a sure sign that your dog is out of control. A slack leash represents a dog that is in control and wants to listen. I do not let my dogs greet other dogs whose owners are pulling tight on the leash. It tells me that they are nervous and inexperienced, and that their dog could be aggressive—which the owner probably caused in the first place.

Solution

Loosen up your leash when you meet another dog. Relax. Your dog looks to you as his leader. You may still hold on to the leash, just make sure that it's slack so that your dog can sniff, wag his tail, lower or raise his head, or give hundreds of other signals to the dog he's meeting. Remember, dogs don't have conversations with their voices, they communicate through body language. Loosen up, and allow your dog to meet and greet properly. Pet the other dog, so your dog can see that it's safe and fun. Say hi to the other dog with a positive "up" voice, and squat down to engage the other dog. Your dog will see and feel you relax into a wonderful greeting ceremony.

When you tighten your lead and hold your dog back, you ignite his opposition reflex. If you pull in one direction, he'll pull harder to get to the other dog, signaling to the other dog in a way that makes him look crazy, unpredictable, or aggressive because you're not allowing him to give proper signals.

Note: This is for normal dogs, with no leash aggression problems. If your dog has a leash aggression problem, a loose leash will not solve it.

HUMAN IMPLICATION

When you keep a "tight leash" on your children, boyfriend, girlfriend, spouse, or even employees, the same "opposition reflex" will occur. Tell your husband he can't do something, and suddenly it becomes the pink elephant. That's all he'll think about, see, or do. A "loose leash" in relationships implies that a bond and mutual trust is inherent. The only reason we keep a "tight leash" on the ones we love is fear. When fear is present, there can be no love or trust.

You're not a bad person for holding the leash tightly, but try loosening up a bit and see what happens. We all know that children reach a certain age where it's time for a little more independence. Parents need to loosen the leash on their children at some point. If you're bonded and you've created mutual trust, respect, and love with the ones you love (including your dog), loosening the leash will bring wonders of joy into your relationships. A dog can't be forced to be good. He should want to *choose* to be good. Same with people.

Don't look when he barks…train yourself!

Your eye contact represents attention and reward for your dog. Remember giving a treat for eye contact? Your dog barks at you because he wants your attention. When you look back, you're rewarding him. This is one sure way to create a barking dog. When your dog is barking at something else (pedestrians, squirrels, intruders, imaginary friends) and you say, "Quiet! No barking!" he just hears you barking along with him. Joining in on the bark fest will only make the barking worse.

Solution

Do not look at your dog when he barks. Instead, next time your dog barks at you or the moon, look away. If he barks again, turn your back. If he's still barking, leave the room without him, and he will begin to realize that his bark has a consequence. It drives you away from him. This is a great consequence because the worst thing is for him to be separated from you. When he learns that his bark causes separation from you and no longer gets him what he wants (a cookie, attention, you joining in on the bark fest), he's likely to become a quieter dog.

By paying attention or giving your dog what he wants for barking, you have actually trained him to bark. If you arrive at your dog's favorite hike, and he's whining and carrying on like mad in the car, do *not* open the door and let him out until he's quiet. Really. It may take twenty minutes, but you'll only have to do it a few times until he gets it. Now your pup realizes he must be quiet to get what he wants.

LEARN TO UNDERSTAND YOUR DOG'S BODY LANGUAGE

This is a very large subject—so large that entire books are dedicated to understanding the nuances and subtleties in a dog's body language. The Internet can also be a valuable resource. But here, I want to cover a few of the basics.

♦ **THE TAIL.** A wagging and loose tail usually means a dog is excited and happy to see you. The tail wagging around in a big circle means, "I'm really happy." When the tail is wagging and stiff or straight up and stiff, this can mean a display of excitement or aggressive posturing and dominance. This does not mean the dog is going to attack, but recognize that it's possible. A relaxed tail at half-mast indicates a dog who is tired, sleepy, relaxed, and non-threatening. If the tail is tucked between legs, the dog is usually terrified, submissive, or unsure. An unfamiliar dog with his tail between his legs means he could potentially bite you out of fear. Don't reach out to pet a dog whose tail is tucked or whose tail is really erect and stiff. Especially if you don't know the dog.

Again, these signals are usually the case, but sometimes we can misread, and a "wagging tail" dog can suddenly attack. Anything is possible.

♦ **THE EARS.** A dog's ears can also be very telling. Erect ears can mean the dog is aroused by something or is listening to you or something else. Erect ears can also indicate a dog who is in attack mode. Keep in mind that "erect" looks different in floppy-eared dogs than it does in stiff-eared dogs. Erect ears combined with an erect tail signifies a heightened state of arousal. Ears pinned back usually indicate fear or submission. A dog with tail tucked and ears pinned back is very fearful or submissive, and he could also be "submissively super happy." I don't think I've ever seen tail tucked with ears perked forward—that wouldn't make sense—but you may see a madly wagging tail with pinned back ears, which means the dog is so happy to see you that he's showing you his submissive ears! And, naturally, a relaxed, non-threatening dog who is just hanging out will usually have relaxed ears.

♦ **MOUTH, LIPS, AND TEETH.** Sometimes a really happy or submissive dog will "smile" and show all his teeth to you. He's not growling or bearing his teeth, he's simply happy to see you. This is good. When I come home, two of my dogs show me all of their teeth. They curl their lips up and expose their canines. This means, "I'm so happy you're home!" I've had many clients believe their dog is growling at them or warning them in this situation, but that's not the case. However, in an unfamiliar dog, lips curled back with teeth showing could be an aggression warning: he's going to bite you if you come any closer. If the mouth is open with the tongue hanging out, the dog is happy, relaxed, or excited.

♦ **THE EYES.** A dog will leer or "stare" at something that he's about to chase, is aroused or excited by, or is aggressive toward. The stare comes before the attack in most cases. The mouth closes, the panting stops, and the dog becomes stiff. If you have an aggressive dog, watch for the "leering." Direct eye contact from an unfamiliar dog means a threat of possible aggression. The dog is leering at you. Direct eye contact from your own pet signifies attention and wonderful obedience. An averting gaze usually indicates submission, fear, or nervousness. And finally, relaxed eyes mean a calm, non-threatened dog.

♦ **BODY POSITION.** An erect, stiff body, usually combined with erect ears and tail, is a likely sign that the dog is unsure, threatened, or going to bite. The dog is saying, "I may need to protect or defend myself, or you." A relaxed dog will have a relaxed body. Sometimes you'll see the wiggle worm syndrome, which means, "I'm so happy to see you, I'm wiggling like a worm!" If the dog takes a fetal position on the ground, it means he is fearful or submissive. When a dog is fearful or submissive, you risk submissive urination and the possibility of fear biting. A urinating dog, however, is usually too submissive to bite.

Remember, any of the above body cues paired with other body cues can mean something else entirely. Do your research, and pay attention to what your dog's body language is telling you.

VOCAL CUES

Bark = the dog wants something (to go out, to play, attention, a squirrel, a toy, food); the dog hears an intruder or visitor.

Growl = a warning that if pushed further, the dog could bite.

Play growl = sounds different than a real growl; used in play fighting. This is great!
Howl = loneliness, boredom, or stress; your dog is waiting for you or calling out to you.
Squeal/yipe = too much rough play, or "the other dog is hurting me."

Dogs in your den are great

Dogs are family animals, and they prefer to live and den together just like we do. When you don't allow your dog into your den, it creates a source of anxiety for him. It can also lead to unwanted whimpering and barking. Many people are taught that allowing your dog to sleep on your bed makes him "dominant." This is in no way true. Each dog is unique, which results in many different possible situations.

Solution

Give your pup a place to sleep in your bedroom. You are his family and partner, and it would be a better quality of life for him to sleep in the den with you.

I love having my dogs in my room, but they sleep on the floor in their own beds. If you want him on your bed, that's fine too. It's up to you whether your dog sleeps on your bed or not. Contrary to some myths, your dog sleeping on your bed has no bearing on his behavior in everyday life. It will not affect his training. What you reinforce, pay attention to, and do not pay attention to day in and day out has every bit to do with what kind of dog you'll create. But when it comes to where your pup sleeps, whether he has excellent or terrible obedience, or whether or not he's aggressive toward you or other dogs—it doesn't matter. Sleeping on the bed has nothing to do with this. Sleeping on the bed is simply sleeping on the bed, and nothing else.

Neuter or spay right away

Neutering or spaying your pup won't change his or her personality. But many things *will* change. Getting your dog fixed reduces or eliminates marking (when males lift their legs on the corners of things). He'll become friendlier and less threatening to other dogs. He won't be so obsessed with sniffing and mounting. And he'll be more trainable and bonded to you, rather than being more interested in his environment. It's actually very hard on a dog to be the only intact male around. Other dogs will not leave intact males alone. They sniff and mount constantly.

If a male dog who isn't neutered "smells" a female in heat, it will drive him crazy, and he'll be terribly uncomfortable. Some dogs even jump fences and dig out of yards in order to find the female—resulting in puppies, which are filling animal shelters across the United States. If you wait too long to neuter your dog, it could cause certain cancer later in life. A female can become very uncomfortable during her cycle, especially if other dogs keep mounting her. This can lead her to become defensive toward other dogs. She may begin to snap at other dogs to keep them away.

Solution

Neuter or spay your dog before he/she reaches one year of age, and preferably before the female's first cycle (usually between six and twelve months). Sometimes, if you notice very early marking and mounting behaviors or signs of aggression, you can spay or neuter immediately. Especially if there is a potential for aggression. Shelters neuter and spay at eight weeks if a dog finds a home. I'm not suggesting you neuter or spay *that* early, but it really will not harm the dog.

My Search and Rescue dog became *more* driven to work after I neutered him. His attention and focus increased, and he was far less distracted. Deer could sprint right in front of him, and he remained perfectly focused on finding the missing person. Of course, this has to do with his training, as well, but there was a noticeable improvement after the neutering.

Physical manipulation

Try never to physically manipulate your dog. For example, don't say, "Sit," and push the dog's butt down. Or don't say, "Down," and pull the dog's front legs out to slide him into position. Dogs will learn to sit because they're avoiding your "push." It's not a very pleasant way for the dog to learn. Instead, see this book's sections on how to lure your dog into basic positions.

Keep your dog cool

Do *not* pour water over your dog's back, especially when he's hot. This creates a steam-bath effect, and the sun beats down on his wet back and actually heats the dog up even more.

Solution

If you can, it's great to fully immerse a dog in water, or wet the feet, chest, and neck of the dog if he's hot. Do not, if you have a choice, pour the water on his back. This will only make him hotter. Also, a dog's fur or hair protects him from the sun. He's able to raise his hair or fur and create a layer of shade for his sensitive skin, which lacks pigment. When you shave your dog or give him too short of a haircut, you actually risk making your dog hotter or sunburned. Your dog's coat protects him from cold and heat. If your dog does get a summer-clip, make sure it's not too short and that the sun can't beat directly onto his skin.

SIGNS OF HEAT STROKE

If your dog is exhibiting any of these signs, get him cool or into the shade, and get him to the vet immediately.

- Huge, extended tongue paired with heavy panting
- Bright red or very bright pink gums
- Vomiting
- Collapsing
- Seizures

Cars are not kennels

Your car heats up a lot faster than you think. Every year, dogs die this way. I knew two people who left their cars running with the air conditioner on, and the car stalled and the dogs died. Remember, your dog has a fur coat on and naturally feels thirty degrees hotter than you do. One of my clients left her dog in the car on a cool day while she ran into the grocery store. When she came out, her windows were bashed in, and someone had "saved" her dogs and turned them in to the pound.

I also know a woman whose car was stolen with her dog in it. She never saw him again. And more than one client has had a dog chew through leather seats, thrashing their cars.

Solution

Never leave your dog alone in the car. There really is no safe way to do it. It simply should never be done.

Prevent a darting dog

Think about it: if you try to grab your dog when you want him to get in his kennel or stop doing something, then your dog will most certainly start to avoid you. In fact, this is exactly how you would teach your dog to avoid you—by grabbing him and putting him in his kennel.

Some dogs have severe avoidance issues. When you go to grab their collars, they duck or run away to prevent you from grabbing them. This is a result of a dog who has fear issues, or a dog who has been "grabbed" when being disciplined, put in his crate, or brought away from other dogs. Pulling your dog away from things can increase the likelihood that he will become a "darter" or an "avoider."

Solution

Be patient, and teach your dog not to dart. If your dog's life is in danger, this is the time to grab him. Other than that, you should be able to call him to "come."

Respect your dog. Small dogs duck away from people all the time because we never "ask" them or reward them for being picked up. When you own a small dog, you tend just to sweep him up into your arms when *you* need him. He will most certainly begin to avoid you. If you owned a 150-pound mastiff, you *couldn't* pick him up; you'd have to respect his size and rely on training commands. Treat little dogs the same way. When you pick up a little dog, feed him at the same time. He learns to *love* being picked up. I also add in: "I'm going to pick you up," so he knows what's coming. If "I'm going to pick you up" means, "I am going to pick you up plus give you a treat," he should love being picked up. But usually, we just sweep our little dogs up when we need them, and they learn to avoid or even growl at us.

Teach your children how to pick up your little dog this way. The dog will learn to love being picked up by the kids. The kids are *going* to pick the dog up anyway, so it's best to prepare your dog so he won't "snap" when being picked up. Have the kids pick up the dog and feed him at the same time. If they're too young to get the timing down, then *you* feed as your child picks up the dog. Immediately put the pup down, and repeat. The dog will learn to *love* being picked up. This helps prevent future potential avoidance issues that can lead to darting and biting.

Remember, the *first* time your dog growls at you or your children, he's usually *rewarded* because we show fear and stop doing whatever it was we were doing. When this happens, your dog is rewarded for growling because he doesn't get picked up or moved off the bed when he growls. Prevent this. Have your younger dog drag a leash around during the day so if you really need him, you can grab the *leash*, not the dog, and lead him away from the danger.

Teach your dog not to dart. Prevent this by getting a handful of treats. At the exact same moment you reach toward your pup's collar, give a yummy treat, and then let go. Repeat. Do ten repetitions, three times a day. Eventually, your dog will look forward to you grabbing his collar. He learns that grabbing his collar means a yummy treat, *not* discipline or removal from something he loves. Then, when you *need* to grab him, he does not dart away from you.

GAME

MOVE AWAY FROM YOUR DOG

Try this experiment. For an entire day, only move *away* from your dog. He will usually just follow you. Dogs do not have voices; they do not tell each other to "come." They simply move away from other dogs to get other dogs to follow. In the wild, a mother wolf just starts walking away—and the puppies follow!

Try just moving away from your dog for a whole day, and see what this teaches you and your dog. Do not talk. Do not turn to look at him or wait for him. When I'm in the dog park or on a fun hike and it's time to leave, I simply have to walk away, and my dogs always follow. I do not call them to come. I just simply go. This is one of the most powerful things you can teach your dog. If he follows you to the door, leave with him on a walk. If he doesn't follow you to the door, go on a walk without him. Carry treats around in your treat pouch. When he follows you, give him a treat every once in a while. But, whatever you do, *do not* move toward your dog for an entire day. Move away. Find a way to incorporate the "moving away" game into your everyday life. When you need your dog to come with you, just move *away*. You'll be surprised how it works.

Diet

Please don't overfeed your dog, especially if you have a piggy-dog. Obesity is a huge problem in the dog world, as well as in the people world. (Note: overfeeding is different than leaving food bowl down all day, which creates picky eaters.) It's important to keep treats healthy. Obesity can lead to diabetes, pancreatitis, arthritis, and heart disease in our dogs.

Solution

Feed your dog a healthy diet. Try vegetables such as cooked green beans, carrots, or peas. I even like giving frozen carrots, peas, or blueberries on a hot day. You can mix veggies into their regular meals, but I like tricking them into thinking that they are treats. Rice, popcorn, and pasta are also great snacks. Rice cakes? Mmmm…crunchy and good. Dogs love them. I also like making broth ice-cubes. Simply cook some broth and pour into an ice tray for a great summer treat.

Look at your dog. Is he fat? Then feed him less or exercise him more. Weigh your dog, and feed according to the dog's weight on the back of the dog food package. If you have an extremely active and athletic dog and you exercise a lot, you may increase the food a little. You should be able to feel a dog's ribs in some breeds, but not all breeds. By controlling food intake, your dog will feel happier and more energetic, and he'll really look forward to mealtimes. Once again, this is very similar to humans. Also, be careful not to underfeed. If you notice your dog is too skinny or low on energy, rule out any possible medical reasons, and then feed him more.

DEADLY POISONS

Poisoning is a common cause for vet visits. Know these common poisons for the safety of your pet:

- ◆ **Antifreeze**. One teaspoon can kill a small dog. It smells sweet to them, so they're very likely to lick some up.
- ◆ **Mouse and Rat Baits.** These cause bleeding disorders that are fatal.
- ◆ **Slug Bait.** Causes seizures.
- ◆ **Dog Medications.** Beware of overdosing or accidental access to pet meds.
- ◆ **Human Meds.** Consult with your vet before giving medications   to your dog.
- ◆ Insecticides. Keep your dog away from areas you know have been recently sprayed.

Poisonous foods

Take the time to learn what foods can be toxic to dogs. Chocolate, for example, is lethal at one ounce per pound of dog. Other foods you'd never suspect to be harmful—but are— include avocados, raisins, grapes, caffeine, onions, garlic, certain mushrooms, macadamia nuts, some baby food (because of onion powder), cooked bones (can cause obstruction or laceration of digestive system), narcissus, oleander, larkspur, iris, lily of the valley, rhubarb, daphne, wisteria, laurel, rhododendron, azalea, jasmine, cherries, some oaks, jack in the pulpit, mistletoe, buttercup, poinsettia, and certain lilies.

Be careful to not let your pet get into any of these things. Keep household cleaners stored safely away, just as you would with a child. Put plastic casing over any electrical cords to prevent your dog from chewing on them. Dog-proof your home as if you had a two-year-old child.

Chapter  5

Vocal

Create a vocal "song" for each cue

People are *way* too conversational with their dogs. Your dog does not speak English. He tunes out most of what you say, unless he's a border collie. Dogs do not listen to conversational tones because 90% of the time (or more), those tones are not directed at them and become meaningless. On top of that, we *sound boring*. When we try to train our dogs with our boring conversational tone, they tune us out.

Solution

Create a special voice, tone, or song for each cue that means you are talking to your dog. Each separate cue should have its own special inflection and sound. Be creative with this—it can be cartoony or just simply different than your normal conversational tone—but be sure that the cue for each command always sounds the same.

Dogs love an exciting, energetic tone. It's like a cheerleader or a good coach. Your voice should be exciting and motivational. Avoid firm tones. People tend to "bark" firm orders at their dogs. This will repel the dog, and he'll be less likely to listen to you. In fact, he may "freeze up" because you are scaring him. You think he's being disobedient, but he probably doesn't understand what you're saying.

I take this tonal training a step further. Every command and cue I have for my dog has a certain "song" to it. My "come" command has the same tone, pitch, and sound *every* time I say it. If I went over to the piano, I could play the two notes that resemble my "come" command, like a song. This way, your dog will never mistake that you are talking to *him*.

Every time you use the "training voice," you need to learn to have a good consequence for your dog, such as food, a liver treat, or a tug toy. I call this "tonal training." This is precisely why whistles work so well with dogs. A whistle sounds the same *every* time. There's no mistake. Try blowing a whistle and following with a treat for one week, and you'll see how powerful the exact tone can be. After a week, blow the whistle. Your dog will come running. The whistle *only* means come for a treat, never anything else. It really makes a difference.

Some people say, "Max, come!" and the next time they say, "Come 'ere, Maxy poo!" and the next time they call, "Here, boy! Here, Maxy? Come here, boy!" This come command is confusing because it's not even using the same words, much less tone. Your dog picks up on your voice cues, and even the slightest difference in tone could confuse him. You need to say the same words in the same order and have a yummy reward *every* time in order for your dog to really learn the command. If you never reward or have a good consequence, it will not work. Eventually your dog will not respond—the same way you'd no longer go to work if they stopped paying you.

Use a nickname

This goes right along with keeping your commands sacred. I always have a silly nickname for my dogs, one that does not mean attention or obedience. My dog's working name (the name I use when I train) is Django. When I just want him to come over to the couch to snuggle, I use a nickname: Yams. Yes, his nickname is Yams. He knows that when I say, "Yammys!" there is no reward, and he can choose to come over or not. This way, it's not the formal, "Django, come!" command every time I'm wondering where he is or if I want him to come. If I say, "Django, come!" it means 100% that there is going to be a reward and something wonderful is going to happen. I use the nickname when I just want him to come over to me informally. No reward.

Keep commands and cues separate and sacred from everyday talk.

Get behavior first, then add the verbal cue

Most people cue or command their dogs to do something before they really have a good idea of what to do. Don't assume your dog truly knows a behavior right away.

Solution

Instead of saying, "Sit…sit…*sit!*" don't say anything. Get your dog to "sit" first. This will really force you to have to use your hand signals and voice mark at the exact moment the dog is in the correct position.

For "sit," make sure your pup is motivated (hungry), and take a yummy treat in your hand. Slowly lift the treat from his nose up and back over his head. He actually has to sit in order to see where the treat went. As soon as you hold the treat in the right place, he should sit. This is called luring. When he sits, immediately voice mark and follow with a treat. If he backs up instead of sitting, don't treat or voice mark. Wait thirty seconds and try again.

When your pup is consistently sitting as you lift your hand up, only then do you add the word "sit," paired with your hand signal. Now he'll begin to learn the vocal cue as well as the hand signal. You can also just wait for your dog to sit. All dogs sit, even if they haven't been rewarded for it. Wait for it to happen, and then reward it every time. He'll automatically sit more because it gets him a reward and attention from you. Now you can start to give the vocal cue.

Have you "poisoned" a command?

The poisoning of commands happens all the time. First, does the dog actually know the command? If you're sure he does and he's not responding, then maybe it's been poisoned. It's never true that the dog is "stupid," "stubborn," or "not listening to you on purpose." Instead, you've probably poisoned the command by using the command paired with negative events.

For example, calling your dog to come and then putting him in his kennel can poison that command. It's not that the kennel is bad, but he'd rather be doing what he was doing when you called him. Now the "come" command is associated negatively with the kennel. Or, what happens when you call the dog to come and give him a bath? Unless the dog loves baths more than anything else in the world, this is a bad idea. You can also poison the "go touch" or "go say hello" command by pairing it with frightening things or people too soon. If "go touch" always means a scary person is around, your dog will soon be afraid of— and choose to not listen to—the command because you've poisoned it.

Solution

Keep commands pure. This is very hard to do, but once you're conscious of it, it becomes easy. This is why it's so important to create vocabulary with your dog. If "come" means everything (like come inside, take a bath, leave the park, come away from fun and other dogs, come away from prey), then "come" will soon mean nothing. Have different words for everything. For example, have a specific command for getting in the car. Every time my dogs jump in the car, I time it and say "go car" as they're jumping in. Now I can say "go car" from anywhere in the house or yard, or even on a hike, and they'll take me back to the car. I do *not*, however, call them to "come" and then put them in the car.

Do you see and understand the difference? What if every time I called your name, I took you away from something you were enjoying? Wouldn't you stop listening to me?

What about this scenario? Bella, a boxer that I train, goes absolutely crazy when you tell her to "sit" on a walk. The owners couldn't understand what had happened. She'd sit just fine in the house, but if you told her to sit on a walk, you were in big trouble. She'd start tugging on the leash, lunging out, and barking. It was wild. I asked the owners when and how they used the "sit" command on a walk. They explained that she always got extremely excited on walks when she saw other dogs, so they began to tell her to "sit" every time she saw another dog. Pretty soon, with no other dogs present, if you told her to "sit" it meant that another dog was near, and she'd go crazy. The "sit" command had been poisoned.

I simply had the owners put her on a "sit" command for a yummy treat every sixty seconds of her walk for the next week, whether there was another dog present or not. Within the week, "sit" meant "sit," and not "there's another dog nearby."

Think about the commands you have with your dog. Are any of them poisoned? What can you do to recondition your dog so that commands simply mean what they say?

Say cues and commands only once

People wonder why their dog doesn't listen. It's usually because he really doesn't understand what you're saying. This happens if you haven't trained him, if your words are never reinforced and have become meaningless, or if you've "poisoned" the cue or command.

Solution

First, be sure your dog understands the cue or command. Often I see a dog who does *not* understand the cue, hearing, "Peanut, sit, sit, sit, sit, sit." The command comes at least nine times, and the dog is still not sitting. This is very bad. Do *not*, under any circumstances say a cue or command more than once. If your dog does not sit the first time you ask, then remove the reward and yourself, by leaving the room for thirty seconds to a minute. Then try again.

Make sure you've actively trained the behavior with a cue or command and have consistently rewarded it with a *valuable* reward. Now, be clear, use your established tone that you've created for the cue, sound happy and energetic, and confidently cue your dog. If he does not pay attention to you, *do not repeat yourself.* Just remove the reward, and yourself, from the training situation. This way, he learns that your words mean action. If he ignores the command, you fly right into *action* by leaving the room, and he's just lost his opportunity to earn a valuable food reward.

Remember, your dog may not be listening to you because you haven't trained enough or properly, or he may not be motivated to work for you. Have you done your job? Proper motivation is up to you, not your dog. You need to understand how to begin training with food when the dog is actually hungry. There are no unmotivated dogs. There is something that motivates each dog. It's your job to figure out what it is, then use it. Prevent having to repeat yourself or correct your dog. If you cue your dog to do something, he should get either a reward or a reward removal. Create attention. Make words count. Do not repeat yourself like I am doing throughout this entire book!

Avoid warning tones

Remember when you were five years old, misbehaving, and your mother would say, "Maryyyyyyyyyyy?" with an upward inflection in her voice? You immediately knew that you were about to get in big trouble! Humans can tolerate and understand warning tones. Dogs can't. Dogs can warn each other or people with their growls, but they are serious about following through with a consequence (biting) if you push them. They act on their growls.

People tend to nag and nag with warning tones. The problem is that often we give warning tones to our dogs when nothing is really wrong, or we continue to give warning tones and never follow through with a consequence. Warning tones make no sense to your dog; they only signal nervousness.

For example, I always see people giving warning tones to their dogs when meeting other dogs. "Maaax? Be nice. Gentle now, Maaaax…," they say with the upward lilt. Immediately, the dog picks up on the warning tone in your voice and knows you are worried and nervous about the situation. Now you've left him to decide whether or not he "likes" the dog he's meeting, instead of just looking to you as an example. What could have been a wonderful meet and greet becomes a tense interaction for the dogs, possibly causing them to growl.

Solution

When you meet another dog, relax your voice and say, "Hi!" to the other dog. Your dog will hear you saying hello to the other dog, cue off of your happiness, and relax and say hello as well. When you see another dog, try saying, "Let's say hello, Max!" in your happiest voice. Watch everyone relax.

HUMAN IMPLICATION

The mistake I see most people making with their children, employees, spouses, boyfriends, or girlfriends is that there is only a warning tone and never a consequence. I was in a toy store when I heard a boy screaming and throwing a tantrum. I could hear the mother saying, "No, you can't have that," referring to a toy. The boy kept screaming louder and louder, and I just knew that somehow this behavior had been reinforced before. The mother then "warned" the boy, "Charlie, no playing when we get home now." I knew he'd end up getting the toy because of how bad that tantrum was. The screaming became so loud, that the mother, red with rage, grabbed the toy and put it in the cart to buy. The mother reinforced the behavior instead of having the simple consequence of "no toy," and that's it.

If you're going to use warning tones with people, then follow through on your warning or else you'll be viewed as a complete wimp. Even by a five-year-old. The same goes for dogs. Don't use warning tones unless you're willing to do something about it. You can warn your dog with a "leave it." If the dog continues to carry on, walk away from the desired object, dog, or person with your dog on the leash. That's always a great consequence—the removal of what the dog actually wants.

Begging your dog

"Siiiiiitttt?" one owner begs, almost as if she were asking the dog a question instead of saying an exciting cue. "Will you pleeeeeaaaasse sit?" The dog won't sit because he probably doesn't recognize this as one of his established cues.

Solution

Get your voice cues down. Confidently and happily cue your dog with the tone that you created for each cue. You should sound more like a cheerleader—excited and happy. Don't ask for a behavior with an upward, question-like inflection in your voice. Your dog picks up on your voice cues and can tell you don't *really* mean it.

STOP NAGGING—SILENCE IS GOLDEN

Practice saying less. Our words become very meaningless to our dogs, and eventually they tune us out. But notice how the words "cookie" and "walk" always have power? Why? Because we usually follow through with the reward.

Don't say so much! And do not nag your dog. "Fluffy, be nice, now stop that, silly…blah blah blah." You can talk to your dog all day, but do not command him and ask him to "come" and "sit" all day long. He will eventually tune you out. Training, cues, and commands are special. Your dog should be as excited about the word "stay" as he is about the word "cookie." If he's not, it means you've said too much, and you've trained too much with no reward for your dog.

See what happens when you are silent with your dog for a whole day. He'll usually start to pay extreme attention to you, wondering "where" your voice went. He will follow you around more. When you finally ask for a "come" or a "sit," watch him jump into action.

Keep commands and cues sacred. Again, you can talk to your dogs all day—they like this, and there's nothing wrong with it. But keep your commands sacred by not using them all day long. Use them when you train, so that they work when you really need them.

Timing is everything

I'll try not to get super irked as I write about this one—it's my pet peeve, for sure. For example, I see people say "sit" to their dog and he sits…and then gets *up* to take the treat. When this happens, the behavior you're actually rewarding is the getting-up part. Learn good timing.

Solution

Reward your dog at the exact moment he does the correct behavior. This is especially important at the beginning of training. 99% of good dog training is good timing. This is why having a voice marker can be so amazing. You simply voice mark with the word ("good!" or "yes!") at the exact moment your dog does the desired behavior, and then follow with a reward. (See voice marker training in Chapter 1.)

Be careful to look at what behavior you are *really* rewarding. It's all about the timing. If you're potty training your pup, you better bring your treats out with you. Most people take their puppy out to potty, the puppy goes potty, and then they go back in for a treat. The dog is being treated for going back inside the house, not for pottying in the correct spot. Instead, bring your treats outside with you. As soon as he empties himself (and I mean the *exact* moment the stream of urine or poop stops), you immediately voice mark, and then he'll run over to you for his yummy treat. When I'm potty training a dog, I actually voice mark and give a treat at the exact moment the stream of urine is coming out. Yes, my puppies eat at the exact moment that they pee in the correct location. They get this "really?" look on their faces. This can be so exciting for the pup that he'll stop his stream of urine to get his cookie, but at least he'll get the point. And then he usually pees again right after. After a few more potties like this, I wait until he's finished peeing or pooping to voice mark, teaching him to empty himself all the way for a treat.

Timing needs to be immaculate! Practice voice marking at the exact moment your dog exhibits the correct behavior.

Cue with a happy voice

Please do not yell "sit!" at your dog. This will only cause him to freeze up and be too afraid of you to sit. Yelling at your dog or puppy really doesn't work. You may *think* it's working because your dog is cowering, but he's cowering because you're screaming at him. He has no idea, most likely, *what* he did wrong. If you yell and scream commands at your dog, he will not listen to you. In fact, you'll repel your dog away from you.

Solution

Prevent having to yell at your dog. Use a happy, friendly voice when cueing your dog, even if you feel upset. He's more likely to listen if you sound happy. And *never* discipline your dog when he finally does what you wanted…or that may be the last time.

The other night, I was taking a walk with my five dogs on leash. A golden retriever from across the street came running toward us. He got to us, and the dogs were just sniffing and greeting, but the owner was so upset and mad that he was absolutely cussing and screaming at his dog to "come." No matter how mad that owner felt, he should have made his voice happy. (Not to mention, it's his fault that his dog was off leash and that it has no proper recall command.) Instead, the stress in his voice drove the dog farther away. Why would a dog come to a screaming, panicked person? When the owner caught up to us, his dog ran away from him because he was scared. Finally the owner was able to catch up to his dog, and he slapped him on the nose. What a great reward for reuniting with his owner. No wonder the dog wanted to run away.

Make sure you're fulfilling exercise requirements, chewing requirements, and socialization requirements. Know what kind of dog to pick if you're getting a new dog. Formally train your dog using voice markers, positive reinforcement, and a lot of love. All of these things should help prevent you from having to yell at your dog. He won't understand what you're saying anyway. If you yell "quiet!" at your dog whenever he barks, he just hears you barking along with him. Pretty funny, huh? Yelling will only make you appear unpredictable and scary to your dog.

Chapter 6

Anthropomorphism

Let your dog be a dog!

Even though you may not want to smell others' urine, your dog does. So many of my clients say, "I hate when he sniffs and pees on everything on our walks," and they want me to "train" their dog to walk continuously.

Solution

Let him sniff! Your dog is a dog, not a human. Let him sniff, pee, investigate, and explore. His greatest pleasures in life come through his nose. Take a walk and let your dog choose which trees, grass, sticks, and things to investigate. Enjoy watching him sniff and explore. I love coming across old items outside in boxes on the curb. I love watching my dogs sniff and investigate the new smells everywhere. He *needs* to sniff and explore.

Let him sniff for at least ten minutes of your walk. If you're just focused on your own exercise or exercising your dog, then plan to stay out longer. Let him sniff first, then take your walk. It's only fair to your dog to be able to experience the wonderful world through his nose. And guess what ends up happening? When you allow him to sniff, he'll end up wanting to walk briskly with you after about ten minutes of investigation. I'm serious. If you *never* let your dog sniff, he'll become obsessed with sniffing, and the entire walk he'll be straining and pulling on the leash because he wants to go over and sniff. Allow him this one harmless and exciting life pleasure.

Remember, it's a relationship. There are two of you. Your dog is more likely to listen to you if you listen to him.

Don't take it personally, your dog doesn't know he did a bad thing

You come home from work to find that your new couch has been transformed into a pile of shredded fluff and fabric. You begin to yell and scream at your dog. He cowers in the corner, terrified of your fit of rage. Well, of *course* he's skulking and cowering away from you. You're acting crazy. And he has no idea what you are yelling about.

I still hear owners say, "Oh, he *knew* that he chewed that couch. You should have seen the look on his face when I walked through the door." The look on his face was because of your reaction to the couch when you walked through the door. No matter how big of a rage you are in, your dog does not understand why you are screaming at him. If you were sitting on the couch and he began to chew the corner of the pillow, you could "catch him in the act," and he'd have a better idea. However, punishing your dog "after the fact" can be very detrimental to your trust and relationship with him. You become a scary, unpredictable, and crazy person in his eyes, and he's even *more* likely to tear something up or soil the house. When dogs experience stress and anxiety, they often can become destructive. Now you've caused him so much anxiety that he'll probably tear up something else.

A dog destroys furniture because it works. It gives him something to do, and he thinks it eventually brings you home. It's a self-rewarding behavior because it's fun to chew things up. Dogs usually destroy things because they are anxious, have a lot of energy, or lack proper chew toys. He's not punishing you or mad at you.

Solution

Prevent destructive behavior ever from happening by giving proper exercise, chew toys, and crate training for when you are gone. If there's a really good bully stick or chewy bone nearby, your dog will choose this over the couch or the chairs. Exercise, mental stimulation, play, crate, schedule, and proper chews—all of these things help prevent bad behavior.

Prevent. Prevent. Prevent. If your dog is destructive and then you return home, he believes his destructive behaviors brought you home, and it reinforces his bad behavior. Using a crate with toys inside ensures that he will not tear up your house and then be rewarded for the destruction by you coming home. That is a big one. Yes, when your dog shreds your shoes and then you come home, he may believe that shredding your shoes made you appear. Separation anxiety is reinforced this way, as well. Your dog barks, claws the walls, and shreds the carpet for four hours straight, and then you walk through the door. He thinks behaving this way caused you to come home, thus reinforcing his panic attack. By preventing the behavior (with use of the crate) he realizes that chewing his toy and remaining calm brings you home; thus, that behavior is reinforced. Prevention is miraculous.

When you find an accident after the fact (poop on your rug, destroyed objects), quietly pick it up. Don't make a big deal about it. You're too late to scold him, and he will not understand. Instead, work on prevention. If you own a pup or a new dog, try crating when you leave. Give proper chews in the crate so he has something to do and looks forward to it. He will learn to become addicted to his proper chew toys and not the couch cushions. Once he starts tearing up pillows, it's very rewarding and hard to change.

Sometimes I give frozen, raw marrow bones to my dogs when I leave. Because they're frozen, it takes twice as long to get the yummy marrow out. Remember, large raw bones are good, and cooked bones are bad. Cooked bones can sliver and puncture the intestines. Large bones, like knuckle or marrow bones, are safe and easily digested by the dog. Kong toys can be stuffed and frozen as well. You can stuff a Kong toy with cheese, peanut butter, chicken, wet dog food…be creative and freeze. This way, it's ready to go, and a great way to prevent boredom and destructive behaviors. If there's nothing better to chew, your dog will chew your couch or wood chairs. Before you leave home, walk your dog or go on a hike or to the park. Tire him out, leave proper chews, crate him if you're "unsure" of what he'll do out of the crate, and gradually build the number of hours you leave the house.

Keep in mind, for severe separation anxiety you need to see a trainer. This can be a very serious problem, which can be helped tremendously by seeing a behaviorist.

By the way, remember my fear of flying? Well, I panic and sweat and worry to death in the air, and then we land safely, and I get off the plane unscathed. Do you think that reinforces my panic attacks? I can't figure out why they haven't diminished over the years. Maybe it's because I'm always reinforced with a safe, happy landing. Biscuits for thought. You are still alive and kicking; therefore, your mind and body know that every single thing you've done up to this point has kept you alive. Reinforcement in the past means it's hard to make changes.

Dogs don't outgrow problem behaviors

Don't wait to see if your dog will outgrow problem behaviors. Jumping, barking, fear, aggression, not responding to commands—your dog will not outgrow these problems. Usually the problems get worse. For example, if your puppy is backing up or retreating from people, this is not a normal behavior, and your pup will not outgrow it. In fact, some fearful pups can turn out to be extremely dangerous and aggressive dogs.

Solution

Take action to deal with the problem right away. One great way to help a fearful pup is to teach him to "go say hello," just like I did with Buddy, the dog who was afraid of people wearing Halloween costumes in Chapter 3. "Go say hello" is taught simply by placing a treat in someone's hand and having your pup go forward and eat the treat. You are now teaching your pup to move forward and go toward his "fears," rather than retreating and being praised for unwanted behavior.

Get a trainer to help you with your fearful dog. Meeting new people is only one of many "issues" that owners think their dogs will outgrow. Dogs only exhibit behaviors that get them what they want. They only do things that work for them. If your dog is barking all day and night, he will most likely keep barking all day and night unless you figure out what is motivating him and rewarding him to do so. It will not go away by itself. You must change the dog's consequence to change his behaviors.

Using the dog's natural prey drive

Your dog is a dog, not a human. Dogs love to chase, find, hunt, shake, and kill. Use the natural prey drive to create great commands. Think about using your dog's prey drive to help reward him for a job well done. For example, "come" means, "Chase me! I'm a moving, running, fleeing rabbit!" Or "down" means you instantly get to "tug" your toy (this is where he "kills" the toy by shaking his head back and forth).

Use your dog's natural instincts to reward him for wanted, cued behaviors.

Chapter  7

Punishment
(and Why It Doesn't Work)

The truth about punishment

First, let's distinguish punishment vs. negative reinforcement. Many people—even dog trainers—get the two mixed up or don't know the difference. Punishment is a way of learning that occurs when an unpleasant or aversive consequence follows a behavior. Examples of punishment include spanking a child or using an electric bark collar on your dog. Every time your dog barks, he receives a static shock from the collar. After being shocked a few (or many) times, the dog learns by punishment not to bark. The behavior (barking) will diminish or decrease. The dog has learned not to bark because bad things happen when he does. I do not use punishment on dogs, or people.

Negative reinforcement is a different way of learning in which a behavior is made more likely to occur because an unpleasant consequence is avoided or removed. Punishment decreases or eliminates a behavior; negative reinforcement increases a behavior.

What I want to stress is that neither punishment nor negative reinforcement are very powerful training tools. Punishment is almost always misunderstood by your dog. He will eventually view you as unpredictable, scary, and dangerous, and he may defend himself against you by using his bite. If you use punishment, the only way it is understood is if the "punishment" happens at the exact—and I mean *exact*—moment that the undesired behavior is happening. Even then, I still don't advocate using punishment. There's a scientifically proven, much more effective way to train.

Punishment and negative reinforcement can have undesirable consequences. Almost always, dogs that receive punishment from their owners become fearful, lose trust, and can develop aggression toward the owner and other dogs. Training becomes a "possibility of being punished" instead of a fun game where fear is not an issue. Also, if the punishment (kicking the dog, scolding the child, garnishing wages) does not work and the incident occurs again, you are then left to escalate the punishment. This can be extremely damaging to the relationship between you and your dog. For example, say your dog misbehaves, and you slap his nose. When he misbehaves again, you hit him harder. The third time, maybe you kick him as hard as you can…and where does this leave you? Your dog really hasn't learned anything except for the fact that you are scary and unpredictable.

One reason punishment does not work is that it occurs after the fact. Animals can't possibly connect the punishment with the bad behavior. Even humans have trouble doing this. If your car died or caught on fire every time you went over the speed limit, you would be much less likely to speed. But instead, the punishment is a fine that is paid long after the fact. And we continue to speed.

Punishment may stop an unwanted behavior, but your dog still has not learned what he *can* do to show improvement. It's much more powerful to use positive reinforcement to increase the likelihood of wanted behaviors.

The dominance myth

Many people have been told that the way to keep a dog in his place is to be more domineering. *Wrong.* This is what I call "The Dominance Myth."

Confronting dominance and aggression with greater dominance and aggression is very damaging to the relationship between you and your dog. It is, in fact, the opposite of a loving, bonded partnership. If you keep getting more and more dominant and aggressive yourself, the dog will get used to it. Then you are forced to be *more* aggressive to get the same results from your dog. What are you going to do? Eventually kick or hurt him? This is *not* the way to solve problems. Your dog will come to fear you and try to escape your touch.

"Domination" is old-school dog training. Today's methods are based in science. Dogs learn like children learn—through love, trust, positive reinforcement, and example. If we simply "act dominant," this only stresses out our dogs. Mine would say, "Why are you acting so stiff? I think I'll go over and pee on the couch because you're making me nervous." Behavior problems *begin* when you start to "dominate" your dog. First of all, your dog knows you are *not* a dog, so to try to dominate him seems ridiculous. Dog "packs" are not viewed as "packs" anymore. The latest research shows that wolves and dogs live in "groups" that are almost identical to human family groups. The wolf "pack" theory is dead. Wolf, wild dog, and domestic dog "groups" are based on cooperation, partnership, mutual trust, bond, and respect. It's not about one single "alpha" who dominates and controls the "pack." You'll never see this in the wild.

Roles change all the time within wolf and dog groups. One may control the food, while the other gets the best sleeping spot. The controlling of resources (food) still proves to be the most similar role to what the "leader" does in the wolf group. We look to the wolf group to understand a little more about our dogs. Keep in mind, our domestic dogs are much different than wolves. In fact, our adult dogs resemble juvenile wolves, and they've been bred to retain these juvenile characteristics (wagging tails, floppy ears). We love those "puppy traits," which puppy wolves exhibit but adult wolves do not. This is called neoteny: the retention of juvenile traits into adulthood.

Don't worry about being the *dominant* leader. Stop dominating your dog into *not* doing. It doesn't work.

Solution

Teach your dog what he *can* do for you. Be the *fun* and *inspiring* leader.

Being the alpha leader will not cure the fear in a fearful dog. Just as being a domineering, bullying parent does not make a child less fearful; it makes him more fearful. How would a father being more strict and firm cure the son's fear? It won't, and it won't for your dog, either.

"Obedience"—change your attitude, change your dog

In SAR (Search and Rescue), where we utilize the most highly-trained dogs, I come across people who have the wrong idea about "obedience." They ask their dog to "sit" or "down" or "drop" on recall, and he cowers as if he were in trouble. The entire word "obedience" is the wrong attitude to have. What if a dog saw "obedience" as fun, exciting, and rewarding—the best part of the day?

Solution

Get the word "obedience" out of your head. Replace it with the promise of fun, games, and excitement, and your dog will want to be 100% obedient. He doesn't *have* to be obedient—he *wants* to be obedient. Your dog should be thinking, "You mean I *get* the opportunity to drop on a recall? YEHAW!!!" The dogs (including mine) who do "obedience" for me do it as if it were the most fun thing they've ever done. And they have near perfect and speedy drops on recall, stays, sits, downs, and heels with perfect attention. Change your attitude to one of *fun*, and your dog will choose you over any distraction.

Chapter 8

Bad Behaviors

There are no bad dogs

Jumping, barking, digging holes, chewing things, mounting, peeing, and growling are all behaviors, not bad behaviors. As soon as you view your dog as "bad," you are placing a judgment on him, and behaviors will be harder to change because of your attitude. I believe that there are no bad dogs. In most cases, I've seen "bad owners" who create bad dogs. By not making the classic mistakes that most people make, you can create a wonderful, well-rounded pet who can change and enhance your life for the better. And you can create a dog who has an outlet to be a dog.

In a few very rare and extreme cases, there can be a dog that is so terribly aggressive (and again, this is due to abuse, neglect, or lack of socialization—and that is a human's fault) that euthanasia is the only solution. This poor dog must now be killed because an owner somehow and somewhere made classic mistakes. Lack of socialization with people and dogs is the number one reason that a dog becomes aggressive and ends up being killed. The only exceptions are if your dog is in pain or has a medical issue that's causing aggression. Aside from those two examples, most bad behavior is created by the owner. *There are no bad dogs*.

Solution

Take this book as a manual or instruction book to help guide you and your relationship with your dog. This should enhance your partnership and make life with your pup much more enjoyable. Believe me, he'll be thankful you read this book.

I always used to wish there was some kind of "manual" for raising children. I thought it very strange, even as a small child, that we didn't come with instructions. How are we supposed to know what to do? Trial and error, I guess. And I see life, both human and animal, as much more important than trial and error. We humans will experience the error, no matter what; the least we can do is get on the right page about what to do, and what not to do, with our pets.

Take action early

People call me with five- and six-year-old dogs (sometimes even older) to tell me of a behavioral problem that's gotten out of control. The longer a dog has a problem, the longer it will take to fix. Do something the minute you see there's a problem. Little things turn into big problems when left alone.

Solution

Get help at the first sign of a problem. If you're not sure there's a problem, most likely there is. Go with your gut. Call a trainer in your area or, if it's minor, go online or read a book about your issues with your dog. Something as simple as a cute puppy jumping up on your leg to try to kiss your face can turn into a 120-pound dog jumping up to accidentally break your nose. Big problems usually always start small. At the first sign of aggression (growling, biting, snapping at children, lunging at other dogs), get help. By getting help early, you are much more likely to be able to cure the problem. Don't be embarrassed by admitting your dog (and *you*) have a problem. The most damage is done by not doing anything about it at all. If your problem is small, begin now.

Figure out the reward

When your dog exhibits an unwanted behavior, the first thing I do is try to figure out what he's getting out of it, and if I can change that, I will. What is his reward? What is he possibly getting out of doing this?

Think about the dog who barks madly at the mailman. What happens? The mailman goes away, and the dog actually believes that his barking drove the mailman away. At the very moment the mailman goes on his way, the dog is reinforced. I teach an alternative behavior. When the mailman comes, if he's tolerant, we can go out and "say hello." My mailman loves to give my dogs treats. If the mailman doesn't want to participate, you can teach your dog to "go to his spot" for a cookie when the mailman comes. First, teach the dog "go to your bed" (or some other spot) by tossing treats onto his bed or spot. Do this, of course, when there is no mailman or distraction around. If you want things to change more quickly, give your dog *all* his food for going to his spot.

After about a week, don't cue the behavior all day. Wait until the mailman comes, and then cue "go to your spot." Usually, if you've trained properly, the dog will run to his spot, even though the mailman is there. Soon, the mailman becomes what's called an environmental cue. The sight of the mailman will cause the dog to run to his bed for a liver treat, if done consistently and correctly.

I once had a client with a beagle who constantly pooped in his cage. Like clockwork, the instant she put Murphy the beagle in his cage, he'd poop. I thought for a few seconds. Ah ha! "What do you do as soon as Murphy poops in his cage?" I asked. "Oh, I take him outside immediately!" This, clearly, was Murphy's reward. "If I poop in my cage, I'll get taken out." In this case, we had to change a lot of things. First, we worked with prevention and timing. We got a second kennel, and after he'd poop, we'd move him from the poop kennel into another smaller kennel. No emotions. Just no reward. If he stayed in the second kennel for five to ten minutes without pooping, we took him out, and gradually increased the time from there. It worked wonders.

Reward the absence of unwanted behaviors

Many people resort to punishment techniques of training because they don't know any other way. They don't realize that unwanted behaviors can be trained *out* of your dog, just like you can train your dog to have wanted behaviors. As usual, the key to desired results is timing and reward.

Solution

Train unwanted behaviors out of your dog by rewarding the *absence* of unwanted behaviors. Attention can be as powerful as a treat. Behaviors will increase when you pay attention to them. Nudging is one, in particular, that most people don't realize they're doing. I've been to a home where the dog was nudging and bumping my hand for attention. When I ignored the behavior, he began to nose jab my leg and just about flipped me off the couch. The owner confessed that he nudges her hand, and she always pets him for it because he's "asking her" for attention. *She* created the nudging behavior, not the dog. The dog was simply rewarded over and over again for his nudging with attention and petting. This is a sure way to create a real pest.

Instead, pay attention to your dog when he's lying quietly by your feet or sitting quietly next to you. If he's already a "nudger," start to ignore it, or let the behavior of nudging drive you right out the door without your dog. When he's *not* nudging you, be sure to tell him what a good boy he is, and add physical petting, even treats. Don't wait until he's "asking" you for attention by barking, nudging, or jumping up. What you pay attention to will stick around. Always pay attention to your dog for sitting quietly by your side.

This works with a barking or begging dog, as well. Hold the yummy or desired item that's causing your dog to whine or bark. Ignore him until he's quiet. As soon as he's quiet, look over, and give him back the object or toy. Completely ignore him until he's totally quiet, then give the reward for the *absence* of barking. Quiet has to be more rewarding than barking, and your dog will choose quiet. But, again, the *quiet* behavior must be rewarded. People forget this part. It's so important to reward the desired behavior. Don't just dwell on the consequence for barking. Reward and pay attention to your dog before the barking begins.

If barking or jumping begins during training, leave the house immediately. You only have to leave for thirty to sixty seconds to get the point across. This is reward removal, and it is extremely powerful. You and the treats are the reward, and you leave immediately and exactly when the undesired behavior begins. Rewarding the absence of an unwanted behavior is a great way to train.

Start young. When your puppy walks nicely by another dog, reward with a treat. If he barks, pulls, lunges, or whines—no treat. He'll learn to choose the treat over the "no treat" option if you play fair! Start immediately with these games before your dog is eighty pounds. Even if he's already eighty pounds, you can still apply these games.

EXTINCTION BURSTS

A lot of times, I suggest ignoring a bad behavior so that it will go away. With barking or jumping, for example, I tell people to ignore it. What will happen is that the dog will bark louder and louder, or jump harder and higher, before he decides that it's not working and quits. The behavior may temporarily get worse before it fades away into oblivion. Keep ignoring. When your dog is having this "extinction burst," that means the behavior is just about to become extinct.

If you pay attention or reward during the extinction burst, you've just given the most powerful form of reinforcement—intermittent reinforcement—and your dog is most certainly going to keep up the unwanted behavior. When the dog is "bursting" and getting worse and worse, remember that he's just about to quit. Be ready. When he finally gives up, pay a lot of attention to him. As I explained earlier, rewarding the *absence* of an unwanted behavior is a very powerful training technique.

Humans act the same way all the time. Let's say you go to a soda machine every day and put your quarters in for a soda. It's always worked in the past, but one day the machine does not work. What do you do? You probably don't just give up and walk away.

At the very least, you jiggle the handle, push the return coin lever, shake the machine, or even resort to kicking and violently cursing the machine. Your behavior got *worse* before you gave up and went away. You may try again the next day, but after a few days, you won't even go up to that machine anymore. Understanding "extinction bursts" will help you work your dog through ignoring unwanted behaviors. Be patient. The worst thing you can do is to give in and pay attention to your dog during an extinction burst.

Put bad behaviors on cue

When a dog has a terrible problem—like barking—that won't stop long enough to give you an opportunity to reward the absence of the behavior, one of the first things I do is to train him to bark. He's already barking all day long. By putting the bark on cue, I then cue him to bark and reward him all day long. I make him bark over and over again. Each day I give the cue less and less, until finally my dog only barks when I give the cue.

This can be done with jumping up, as well. My Aussie had a terrible jumping problem, so I taught him to "hup-up," which meant to jump up on my chest. I told him to "hup-up" for two weeks straight. Jumping was then phased out by giving the cue less and less, and now he only "hup-ups" to give me a hug, and it's a very cute trick.

Dogs love to dig. Digging is a self-rewarding behavior because the dirt feels cool and nice to lie down in, and digging is fun. It expends energy and gives the dog something to do. One of my clients had a chocolate lab named Barkley that dug ten to twenty holes in their backyard each day. I had them build a sandbox in their backyard and teach Barkley to dig there on command. Digging became Barkley's job. Having a "digging box" or sandbox and teaching a dog *where* to dig can be incredibly fun. Dogs love to dig in sand. Naturally, as soon as he felt the cool sand on his paws, he began to dig. We voice marked, treated him, and said, "Good dig!" Pretty soon, when you said, "Go dig" to Barkley, he'd run to the sandbox and dig. The holes in the lawn stopped completely.

Practice new behaviors, not old ones

We spend five minutes, six times a day, training our dog not to bark and lunge at other people and dogs. That's thirty minutes of solid training per day. We think we're doing a great job. However, when we leave for work, Charlie is at the bay window "practicing" his old ways. He spends hours every day barking at birds, squirrels, other dogs, and people from the window, behavior that is reinforced as he watches them be driven away. This can't happen. If he's practicing his old ways all day long, your training will not hold up.

Solution

Prevent your dog from practicing his old ways. Maybe this means crate training for a few weeks (or as long as it takes). Give him a yummy raw marrow bone in his kennel, and increase your walks and exercise at the same time. Or, take him with you whenever you can. Whatever you do, you cannot give your dog the opportunity to practice his old ways, or it will defeat the purpose of all your time spent training.

Stalking the cookie jar

Don't reward your pup for staring at the cookie jar. It may seem cute at first, but I've seen this turn into an all day bark-at-the-cookie-jar-a-thon. Suddenly, it's not cute anymore.

Solution

Give him a cookie for sitting or doing a trick for you instead. If your dog is making strange noises at the cookie jar or his food cabinet, do not mistake this as "he's hungry" and give him a cookie. This only reinforces the behavior. If the behavior never gets him a cookie, eventually he'll stop repeating the behavior.

Can you get your dog off your bed?

I've had owners who think it's cute that they can't get their dogs off the bed. It's actually very dangerous, especially if you have kids who may not heed the warning of a growl.

One of my clients had an apricot toy poodle named Peppy. And Peppy he was. They called me because they could not get Peppy off the bed. He would bear his teeth and growl at them, and they were scared of him, thinking that Peppy may bite them. They had every right to be scared. Peppy was eventually going to bite them. Each time they tried to get Peppy off of the bed, he'd growl and end up getting to stay on the bed. Peppy is not an aggressive dog—his behavior of growling had been consistently rewarded. We viewed Peppy as aggressive because he growled, when the owners actually trained him to growl by reinforcing the dog and leaving him on the bed.

Solution

I put the owners and Peppy on a hand-feeding schedule to help build proper bond. I also did some basic training with Peppy and the clients (he had no training at all before I got there). They lived on the beach in Malibu and never let their dog free to run and play with other dogs because they were scared he'd get hurt or run away. His extra cooped-up energy made him want to hold tight to his beloved position on the bed even more.

I had Peppy wear a leash, and instead of asking Peppy to *please* get off the bed, I told them to grab the very end of the leash and tell him the word "off" as they gently pulled him off the bed using the leash. As soon as he was on the ground, I had them voice mark, "good" or "yes," and treat. This, paired with proper exercise, chew toys, and training, cured Peppy's bed aggression. If Peppy was on the bed, soon, all they had to say was "off," and Peppy would happily jump down off the bed, eventually even for no reward. There are many ways to do this, and if you're unsure about it, talk to a professional trainer in your area.

What to do about begging

When people come to my house, they simply can't believe that all my dogs lie ten to twenty feet away from my dinner table. "How did you train your dogs to do that?" they ask.

Solution

It's simple—I feed them from the table all the time. What matters is how and when you feed them, and where you "throw" the food.

I started off with my dog at my feet, "begging" while I ate dinner. I never fed him. After a few nights, he gave up and went off to lie down. At that very moment, I reinforced him for moving away from the table by throwing some of my food over to where he now was, away from the table. He decided to lie down about ten feet from the table, and every now and then, I threw a morsel of food to reinforce him for being in the correct place. I made being ten feet away from the table more valuable than being right under the table.

Keep in mind, your dog will eventually find crumbs and will be reinforced for begging, unless you give a "larger crumb" for being away from the table. So, you can feed your dog human food from the table, as long as he's in the position that you want him. Simple as that.

I now have three dogs who choose to lie about twenty feet from the table. I throw a scrap to each dog at the end of the meal. It works perfectly, and it's rewarding and fun for the dogs. We also do this when guests come over. We play the "If I'm far enough away from you, you'll throw food" game. I tell my guests to feed my dogs for being across the room. I actually have them throw food if my dogs are on their beds. By the end of the party, all the dogs are on their respective beds, hanging out.

Remember, the dog will always choose the most rewarding scenario. If you don't treat him for proper and wanted behaviors, then he will beg and wait for a few fallen crumbs anyway. You choose, or else your dog most certainly will.

Four feet on the floor is more rewarding than jumping

Think about it…. How will your dog learn not to jump unless he gets to figure out that jumping won't get him anything? If you always use a leash or voice command to prevent him from jumping, then when he's off leash or when you're not looking, he'll surely jump.

Solution

Teach your dog that keeping four feet on the ground produces better results. With your dog on a leash, have someone come to your door and ring the bell (this is best with someone the dog knows, loves, and *always* jumps on). Have them walk in and squeal at the dog. As *soon* as the dog jumps up, the person runs back out the door.

Repeat the entrance again. If the dog jumps again, your friend madly runs out the door and leaves. Soon your dog will become tired, and he'll eventually figure out that jumping up is what's causing all the fun to run out the door without him. As soon as he doesn't jump when the person enters, voice mark with "yes," treat, and have the guest stay a while and play with the dog.

It's the "all four feet on the ground" rule, and once the dog learns it, he gets a treat, or a scratch on the head. The dog jumps because he wants to be up near your face. (Dogs lick their leaders' mouths and faces. Young wolves lick their mother's mouth to "ask" her for food. This causes the mother to regurgitate food for her pups. The behavior of wanting to lick and be near your face has been retained from the wild.) So, as a reward, when he doesn't jump up, get down on his level—actually squat or kneel down—and let him kiss you. This will be very rewarding for him.

In other words, your dog needs to jump in order to learn not to jump. If you always prevent jumping by holding him back and never letting him go forward toward a guest, he'll never learn. You can also actively teach an alternative behavior in its place. Be creative. Tell him to "sit" for a guest. Or "go say hello" can mean go take food from guests' hands *only* after he's sitting.

Stop laughing—even though mounting your leg is funny

You may think it's funny and entertaining when your dog mounts somebody's leg. And it is...or maybe not. Regardless, it's bad manners, and by laughing you're encouraging and reinforcing a behavior that most people won't like—and most dogs won't like it either. When your dog hears you laughing at him for certain behaviors, he sees this as attention, and he will exhibit that behavior more and more. Remember, attention is a reward, and it reinforces behavior.

Solution

Don't laugh at unwanted behaviors. Ignore your dog's mounting, or leave the house. Teach him that mounting means you will actually leave without him. Everyone in the family has to play by the same rules. Remember, when a behavior is sometimes reinforced and sometimes ignored, that is the most powerful way to maintain a behavior. That's intermittent reinforcement, or gambling, and it encourages the dog to keep trying because he knows that sometimes it will work. To end an unwanted behavior like mounting, it must always cause him to be separated from you. The removal of the reward will teach him that mounting never gets him what he wants.

Manage neurotic behavior

A client who owns a brussels griffon named Spam had gotten himself into trouble. He rescued Spam, who had been cooped up in a kennel most of his life (which is an incorrect use of the crate). Spam developed a really bad spinning behavior where he'd pace back and forth and then spin madly in circles like the Tasmanian Devil. Everyone thought it was cute, and they even gave it a name. "Spin!" they would shriek madly as the dog would wind himself in tighter and tighter 360-degree spins. This amounted to the whole family helping reward and encourage a neurotic behavior. When the dog is spinning, he's feeling anxious. It's similar to picking your nails; you do it when you're worried about something. By rewarding this behavior, it made the dog spin more and more, until that's almost all he did until he went to sleep. That's when they called me.

Solution

Ignore neurotic behaviors and teach alternative tricks. It's important to remember that ignoring your dog won't cure all his problems, but it's a great way to diminish or make a behavior extinct. I told Spam's owner simply to ignore the spinning behavior, and within two weeks, it was almost entirely gone. And the dog seemed much calmer and happier. Spinning can be a really cute trick, but in this case, Spam's spinning was a result of boredom and being locked in a cage. Also, Spam would only spin when he was really scared or nervous. It would be better to teach Spam new tricks, like "roll over" and "shake a paw," instead of rewarding the nervous spinning behavior.

New behaviors are a great alternative to disciplining behaviors you don't want. Give an outlet for your dog to be a dog! Tricks are very fun to teach your dog. If you have some time on your hands, pick up a book on trick training. This can be extremely fun for you and your dog, and you'll be amazed at how smart your pooch is. This also gives you a fun time together, helps to build trust and bond, and it gives your dog a job!

You walk your dog; he doesn't walk you

When your dog pulls you down the road, it's very annoying. It makes for a very unpleasant walk, and your dog is really not getting any more exercise this way. Like we've done in previous examples, ask yourself the question, "What is the reinforcement? What is my dog getting when he pulls me?" The answer is: he's getting closer to what he wants. If he pulls on his leash when he sees a dog ahead, and you simply continue toward the other dog, he's just been rewarded for pulling. He learns, and is actually being trained, to pull you.

Solution

Teach your pup a new consequence for pulling. When your dog pulls on the leash, immediately walk in the opposite direction. The instant you feel tension on your leash, do a 180-degree turn. Walk in the opposite direction for ten brisk steps, then turn back toward the object of desire. If he pulls again, turn around again.

Teach your pup to "heel." Start in the house, with *no* distractions. "Heel" means "walk by my side" (preferably without switching sides). Start by luring your dog with a yummy treat right by your side. Say "heel," voice mark, and treat when he's in the exact, correct position. I begin in the house with my dog off leash to teach the word and position for "heel." If my dog gets ahead, I simply change directions. I make it into a fun game, where he ends up choosing to be in the correct "heel" position. Try to feed him by your side as you continue to walk. When my dog is heeling in a straight line and has this behavior correct 80% of the time, I begin to add turns, figure eights, and direction changes. I treat every time my dog stays by my side. Wear your treat pouch for this exercise, voice mark, and treat when your dog is in the heel position.

Now, when your dog has gotten better at turning and changing directions with you, begin to go longer and longer without a treat. Build the amount of time your dog can heel before getting a treat. If you wait too long without rewarding him, he'll "quit," and that is the delicate balance that you have to create with your dog. Treat a lot in the beginning. Every five to ten paces, he should get a food reward. Don't forget to say "heel" (voice mark) when he's in correct position, and follow with a treat. If he gets ahead of you, do a quick 180-degree pivot turn and walk the other way.

Now you're ready to put these two exercises together outside. Have a friend help you with his dog. We will use the other person and dog as reinforcement (this assumes your dog really likes them; it won't work as reinforcement if he's scared of the person or other dog). Place them about a block away. Begin by saying "heel." Walk out toward the other dog and person. If your dog gets ahead of you, do a 180, take ten steps in the opposite direction, and then turn toward what he wants again.

Keep repeating until he realizes the only way to get to his friend is if he's by your side. When he's "heeling," you continue forward toward what he wants. If he gets ahead of you, you get farther away. Your dog is reinforced by staying by your side and receiving treats when he's in the proper position. And finally, he gets to see the other dog and play. Your dog thinks, "Oh! If I stay by your side, I get closer to the excitement and the other dog. But if I pull ahead, I get turned away from the other dog." If the excitement of the other dog is too much, practice outside without other dogs. Raise the bar slowly, so that your dog has success.

Change what something means

Remember, consequences drive behavior. Often, eliminating bad behaviors can be as easy as changing the consequence of an unwanted behavior. If you pup no longer finds the bad behavior rewarding, he'll stop.

Zipper, a crazy terrier mix, loved to hump everyone's legs. This would cause a fit of screaming and running from the children, and the dog was extremely excited (and thus, rewarded) by the reactions from the children. I told the family to pretend that "humping" meant Zipper wanted to be put outside by himself. For three days, every time Zipper humped, they simply put him outside the sliding glass door, completely separate from the family. Within the three days, the behavior completely stopped. Humping had a new consequence: it meant go outside. And the humping behavior stopped.

Here's another example. Every time I pick up a tennis ball (or anything off the floor at all) my Aussie sprints madly away from me in anticipation of the "throw." I thought to myself: how dangerous. Every time I pick up a ball, a stick, or even my keys, my dog thinks I'm going to throw it for him, and he runs away from me in anticipation to catch the toy. This leaves me out of control and completely far away from my dog. Wouldn't it be great if I taught my dog that picking up a ball, toy, or stick meant run *toward* me?

That's what I set out to do. I first taught my dog to go through my legs by luring him with a treat. I'd say the word "through," as he'd pass under my legs for the yummy treat. Soon, I switched to a ball. When I first picked up the ball, he ran out and away from me (the old behavior) until I said, "through." He ran back toward me (the new behavior), went through my legs (the new behavior), and got rewarded by me throwing the ball for him. Never again did picking up a ball mean run away from me. It's really a safety issue. Training your dog to run toward you for a ball toss can have tremendous power. Now you have a dog whose focus is running toward you, not away from you.

Let your dog choose his own fate and outcome. A really pig-like chow mix I know named Eugene used to bark and whimper and whine at the table for food. We decided to leave the leash on Eugene, and as soon as he made even one small vocalization, we would grab his leash, lead him unemotionally away from the table, and tie him to a sofa-chair across the room. If he was quiet for a few minutes, we'd let him loose again to come back for another try at the dinner table. Again, the instant he barked, we took him back to the "tethering post" sofa. Within two nights, Eugene did not bark at the table anymore. He would rather stay quietly by the table than be tethered far away from it. Eugene chose not to bark because the new consequence for barking was sofa tethering, which he didn't like.

Chapter 9

Education

Want a quick fix?

There's no magic wand for dog training. It takes hard work, common sense, education, and serious training. There is no quick fix for a dog that has not been trained, and especially for a dog who has any sort of problem. If your dog has had a problem for two years, chances are, it may take two years to fix it. TV shows make it seem like your dog can have a complete turnaround in thirty minutes, but I personally have had my own show and have been behind the scenes. Editing is the real magic.

Solution

Be patient. Rehabilitation of an aggressive dog can take several months to several years, and still, chances are high that he'll resort back to his old, aggressive behavior. Training takes *time* and *education*. I've seen examples of dogs who change very quickly. Sometimes it can seem like magic, where a simple change in your own behavior will indeed change your dog very quickly. But more often it can take weeks, months, or even years. Don't let any trainer or TV show lead you to believe there is a quick fix. There's a big difference between entertainment and dog training. Don't be fooled.

Develop a "release" cue

This can save your dog's life. A release cue is what your dog is waiting for. It lets him through doors and off curbs, releases him from a "sit," "down," or "stay," and lets him out of the car. Eventually, he will automatically wait for his release cue in order to go free. The biggest mistake is to teach "sit" or "down" or "stay" without first having a release cue.

A release command is usually the word "okay," and it means your dog can come out of a "sit," "down," or "stay" position, or cross a boundary. If you or your dog does not understand release, then you should not go on to teach "stay" or boundaries.

Solution

Develop a release cue. I've discussed the release command in previous chapters, but it's worth repeating. Here are a few games that will help develop a great release cue.

GAMES

THE FRONT DOOR GAME

Open the door, and hold your dog back using the leash. You go through the door as you hold your pup back inside the boundary. Add a food treat for your dog being inside, and then let him through as you say "okay." Do not give him a treat for being released through the door. You want to build drive and reward for staying behind the boundary, not for being released. Being released through the door is reward enough.

I never, from the very beginning, let my dog out the front door unless he stops at the boundary and waits for his "okay." To be safe, this behavior must first be taught on leash.

THE "STOP"/"OKAY" GAME

I also play the "stop, okay" game to help teach the concept of "okay." This will help your dog understand release. Go outside with your dog on a leash to a relatively non-distracting area. Walk briskly as you say, "Okay." Walk for about ten seconds, and come to a quick, complete stop as you say, "Stop," and freeze. If he "freezes" with you, give him a treat. Freeze for at least ten seconds, then, with a sudden burst, say, "Okay," and begin to move again. You are "releasing" him from the "freeze" position.

THE "SIT"/"RELEASE" GAME

Now, try adding a release to your "sit" command. Tell your dog to sit, and release him with an "okay" before he decides to get up. Eventually he'll learn to "sit," until you "release" him with "okay." Try it with "down," until he starts to get the point. Do this on leash; if he releases himself, getting up before you say "okay," you need to say "no" or "wrong answer," and then you can bring him back to where he got up and redirect him to "sit" with no second reward. When your dog is on a "sit," waiting for his release, give multiple rewards for attention and eye contact, then release him with an "okay."

THE TREAT TOSS GAME

Another game to help teach the concept of "okay" is to throw treats. Get a handful of yummy treats, and throw them as you say the word "okay." Let your dog run after the treats. Now, say "sit" as you throw a treat. He most likely will run after it. Hold the leash and gently restrain him from being able to reach the treat, or walk your dog farther away from the treat, and ask for a "sit" again. Once he sits, I finally release him with an "okay" to run and eat the other treat that I threw on the ground.

Train a thinking dog. If I say "okay," it means run after the treat. If I say "sit," it means sit, and do not run after the treat until I release you with an "okay." All of these games help teach your pup to wait for his release cue. It's like a child in school. You can't just stand up and walk out of class in third grade. You need to raise your hand and ask to be excused by the teacher. Your teacher tells you when it's okay to leave the classroom and go to the bathroom. If our children do this, most certainly our dogs should. Now your dog is the student, you are the teacher. He must not release himself from sit, down, or stay ever again. He may not release himself through any boundaries without you saying "okay." Eventually, it becomes automatic. When you go through a door, your dog will look at you and wait to be "released."

Teach your dog to "drop"

Dogs will "guard" bones or food (resource guarding) as well as toys, underwear, sticks—you name it, a guarder wants to guard it. This can be very dangerous. Most bites happen around the food bowl and bones. If your dog has resource guarding issues, and you suspect real aggression, or you are scared, hire a trainer. Do *not* attempt these methods if you are unsure of your dog's inclination to bite.

Let's begin with a puppy, since puppies are not capable of true aggression. Get a handful of yummy treats. Throw one of his favorite toys, like a cow hoof or a bully stick—something you know he'll love to have in his mouth. If he doesn't put it in his mouth right away, you may have to wear your treat pouch and wait for him to have something in his mouth.

Next, when the toy is in the dog's mouth, have a yummier treat in your hand. Put the treat at your dog's mouth, right in front of his nose, and say "drop" when he smells the yummy treat. He must drop the cow hoof or bully stick in order to eat the treat. In the meantime, you pick up the bully stick. When he's done chewing his treat, give him back the bully stick. It is very important that you give him back the toy during training so he learns to willingly give up his toy for a treat. In order to properly play this game, you must always have the higher value item in your hands.

Mental stimulation

Your dog is bored. I know, you're a great owner; but still, he's bored. After a really good mental training session, my dogs are exhausted. Clients call me after training lessons and tell me that their dogs slept for hours. Brain exercise can tire your dog out almost as much as physical exercise. I'm always shocked when I see how small most dogs' vocabularies are. I also can't stand when a dog walks around a post on a leash and can't figure out how to get untangled. This is the owner's fault, not the dog's fault.

Solution

Start by naming everything your dog does. This will help create understanding between you and your dog. As he's chasing his ball, say, "Get the ball." When he's drinking water, say, "Drink water." As he crosses the threshold of the door to go out, say, "Outside." Soon, when you're just sitting on the couch and you say, "Outside," your dog will run to the door. He's learned the word.

My dog knows hundreds of words, concepts, and commands. He knows the difference between his pink elephant and his purple dinosaur. He can't really see the colors; he just knows which is which from naming them. I can say "go car" from my living room, and my dogs all run to the car. My Aussie even carries my cooler to the car for me. He also skateboards and gets me a beer or a water from the fridge. My chow mix Eugene knows how to sneeze on command and then fetch a Kleenex.

Why stop at just three or four commands and words? There's no limit to how many words a dog can know. Does your brain fill up at a certain amount of words? I don't think so. A very famous border collie named Betsy graced the March 2008 cover of *National Geographic*. She is six years old, her vocabulary is 340 words and counting, she can put names to objects faster than a great ape, and at ten weeks of age she knew all her basic commands and was rushing to retrieve objects by name: ball, rope, keys, and dozens more. She knows at least fifteen people by name, and in scientific tests she's proved her skill at linking photographs with the objects they represent.

How creative can you be with your dog? The sky is the limit. A good mental training session is great for you and your dog. Start with two toys, and give them both a name. When you throw the ball, say, "Ball," and when you throw the rope, say, "Rope toy." Soon, he'll know the difference between the two, and you can add a third. You can even stand by with a bag of treats, and when he gets the correct toy, reward him with a yummy snack. And keep in mind, even training basic obedience is also a great mental workout.

HUMAN IMPLICATION

Humans suffer from a lack of mental stimulation as well—too much TV, computer, and texting. Get outside, go listen to an orchestra, go to a museum, see a play, or read a book. It will enhance your creativity, inspire you, and ignite your passion.

Sitting in front of the TV produces approximately the same brainwaves as sleeping. Tragic. Stimulate your mind—you'll find magic there.

Don't pair your dog's name with negatives

No wonder your dog won't come when you call him. "Max, come!" means any one of the following things may happen: you're leaving somewhere fun; it's time for a bath; come inside so I can put you in your cage because I am leaving; don't do that; time to clip your nails.... You get my drift. Don't ever use the word "no" paired with the dog's name, and don't ever use the dog's name to scold him. We ruin our dog's name by pairing the name with things he doesn't like. So, when you say, "Max, come!" he probably won't.

Solution

Create a productive vocabulary for you and your pup. Use "in the house" or "kennel up," as you throw a treat into his kennel. When it's time to leave somewhere fun, instead of using your dog's name to call him to "come," say, "Let's go to the car!" Always have a treat for him when he gets in. Or you can teach "This way" using the leash. Change directions quickly as you say, "This way," and then treat him for changing directions. When it's time to leave someplace fun, run alongside him and then quickly switch directions and say, "This way!" You'll see him follow you right out to the car.

We tend to use our dogs' names for everything, and therefore it begins to mean nothing. Instead, work on training specifics. When I say, "Take a bath," my dog runs to the hose. We have fun with it. I used a few pieces of cheese during our first gentle baths, and now he loves them. I save his name for anything that is good. Use the dog's name when it's time to eat or have a new toy. Use the name when you're about to go out with him on a walk. These things will reinforce that his name is good, and when you call him to come or say his name, he will pay attention.

HUMAN IMPLICATION

I've literally seen wives train their husbands to "ignore" them. I have a very good married friend, whose name will remain a secret. I was invited for dinner at her home. Every time she said her husband's name, she would nag, nag, and nag. She would call his name and immediately start to complain about all the things that were going wrong. Soon, within one hour of my being there, the husband completely ignored the wife's calls. In fact, he even looked over at me and rolled his eyes when she called his name.

Do not nag your husband, child, or dog. Soon, they will all ignore you or even rebel. Use positive reinforcement. Be super nice, and then ask for what you need. Maybe you'll even put on that sexy nightgown that your husband likes if he'll help you out—believe me, this is much better than nagging. You nag because you want something; why not offer a reward instead? Everyone will be happier. What is so wrong with that?

First teach without distractions

So, you think your dog does "sit," "down," "stay," and "come" perfectly in the living room? This in no way means that he will be able to do these in the middle of the dog park or off leash. Don't have unrealistic expectations.

Solution

Train commands in a distraction-free setting until your dog knows them extremely well and can perform them consistently; then, gradually begin to add distractions.

Try training in the home when a friend (a human friend) comes over. This adds a new level of distraction. If that goes well, take it to the backyard, and then the front yard. If he can't pay attention in the front yard because it's too distracting and exciting, move to the backyard for a few more training sessions. Eventually, have another dog over in your home. With the other dog on a leash and under control, begin to train your dog. He'll learn how to come away from the other dog. Your dog should be on leash as well, so that if he "decides" not to come, you can follow through by gently pulling him toward you, keeping your voice happy, voice marking, and treating when he gets to you. Then, as part of the game, let him go back over to the other dog for play. Practice calling him over to you again. He eventually learns that coming to you is fun; he gets a treat and then gets to go back to playing with the other dog. This is just one example of how to gradually introduce distractions and have your pup still listen.

When he is not listening, move to a less distracting area. Make sure he's motivated for the treats or play toy that you have for his reward, or don't attempt to begin training with distractions. A dog must practice and learn how to come away from distractions such as food, other people, other dogs, squirrels, etc. It's very powerful in training to reward him and then *let him go back to what he was doing*. If coming to you always means the fun is ending, then he'll eventually stop coming to you. Remember, set up distraction trainings only after your dog is 80% consistent in the home. Go slowly, and gradually introduce new distractions.

"No" is a good word

I like to use "no." People have fits with this. "No" is not a bad word unless your dog has been punished using that word. I never use the word "no" as punishment. I teach "no" as a game. No does *not* mean anything scary. It simply means "wrong answer"—it simply means *no*. If you took a kid into the candy store, and he asked for 200 pounds of candy, you would simply tell him, "No, that's too much candy." It does not mean he's in trouble, it simply means, "No, you can't have all of the candy in the store."

Solution

Teach your dog what you want the word "no" to mean. Your dog actually can learn to love the word "no" if you reward him for responding to the word. It's simply a concept, and dogs are capable of conceptual learning.

I teach "no" by playing a game. Start out by holding the leash with your dog standing up. Throw a treat across the ground so that it rolls, making the dog want to chase the treat. As you throw the treat, say, "Okay," in a very sing-songy voice. He will love this part of the game, where you throw treats and reinforce his release word "okay." After about five "okays", show him the treat and say the word "no," and then throw the treat. If he goes for it, simply restrain him from being able to chase the treat while repeating the word "no." You should hold the leash ever so gently, preventing him from chasing the treat, or you can block him with your foot. Here's the fun part—when he finally stops trying to get the treat, then you give him another treat right there from your hands, rewarding the behavior of *not* chasing the treat you just threw. Then, release him with a happy "okay" to go and get the treat that you threw. Don't be hesitant if your dog is hesitant. Show him what to do by being physical with your body. Run toward the treat, point at it, and happily repeat saying "okay" until he gets that it's okay to eat it.

The dog eventually understands, "Oh, 'no' means do not chase the treat. If I listen and do not chase the treat, I get a *better* treat from my owner's hand, and then he releases me to get the very treat that he threw in the first place!" Your dog will double his reward if he listens to the "no." "No" eventually means, "Stop what you're doing and look at me." Your dog earns a food reward for not chasing the treat, and he'll wait for his release cue to go and get it. This game can be really fun.

Eventually, you can throw a tennis ball. Your dog will want to chase and chase. Simply hold the leash a little tighter, and throw the ball as you say, "No." Keep in mind he's on a leash, and you're simply preventing him from chasing a ball. When he pays attention to the "no" and does not chase the ball, that's when you should release him to then go and get it. He learns to stop when you say "no," and then he receives a double reward: a treat plus getting to eventually get that same ball. You are training a thinking dog. Why is this important? What if your dog is chasing a ball, and you need to stop him for some reason? You want to have a dog who understands when to chase or not to chase.

"No" does not mean "bad." In fact, it usually means, "Look at me until I treat you or release you to get what you were going after." If you train this properly, dogs actually love the word "no" because it's a chance to earn an extra treat. You need to practice; one training session is not enough. Practice five minutes three times a day, until he's really stopping on a dime when you say the word "no."

The other great thing about "no" is that it serves as a "no reward" word. All the games where we use no reward (reward removal) can also be paired with the word "no." For example, if you are holding a yummy treat and the dog jumps, say, "No," and turn your back. Turn toward the dog again, and if he doesn't jump, give the treat. Teach this concept and train this as a game. Once he gets the game it can be incredibly fun.

After the dog understands the concept of "no" in the context of these games, you may begin to use the word for "wrong answer" situations. For example, if I say, "Stay," and my dog walks a few steps, I can now say, "No," move him back to where he first moved from, and then repeat, "Stay." He should now understand the concept. Eventually, if he breaks boundaries, jumps up on people, or gets up on your new couch, you can simply tell him (without yelling at him) the word "no," and it will help him learn the rules. "No" should be the last resort to "control" behavior. Work instead on teaching alternative commands. For example, instead of waiting for your dog to jump up on a guest and then telling him, "No," teach him what he *can* do. Teach him to "go say hello" or to "sit" for a cookie in front of the guest, rather than always saying, "No," and nagging your dog.

ESL—ENGLISH AS A SECOND LANGUAGE

Words are just words. Your dog does not understand the difference between the word "no" and the word "good." It's the consequence you provide for these words that teaches your dog to understand. A word is not "bad" or "good," it's only what you make of it. I once saw a comedy act where a man taught his dog to do the opposite of what he was saying. "Come" meant "stay," and "stay" meant "come." "Sit" meant "roll over," and "roll over" meant "sit." It was hilarious, and it proved a great point. Dogs do not speak English. I once taught a dog only French. This didn't mean he understood French; he simply understood the words I taught him, which happened to be French. When it comes to language, dogs understand what we create for them. Be open-minded.

Teach hand signals

I'm always shocked at the number of people who've actually "trained" their dogs without any hand signals. Some people have incorrect hand signals, and others don't even know they exist. Using hand signals can make it easier for your dog.

Solution

Teach your dog proper hand signals. Hand signals are magnificent. My Aussie knows twenty or more separate hand signals. I don't have to say anything at all. It's wonderful.

First, you must know and understand what hand signals are and why they work. For example, when you hold and move your "lure" hand in a certain way, almost all dogs will "sit." Try it: lift a treat high over your dog's head. Most dogs will sit. Therefore, the hand signal for "sit" is a hand up and over the pup's head. To teach a hand signal for "down," bring the treat to the pup's nose and then right down to his feet. Most pups will lie down to try to get the treat. Eventually you can stand up straight and do the hand signal up high, and your dog should understand to go down.

Why have your dog guess if you're talking to him? Let there be no mistake about it. If he hears the cue and sees the hand signal, it's clear to him what you want. It's only fair to him to have a hand signal and a vocal cue combined. It makes it easier for him to understand you. Eventually, if it's extremely noisy or your dog is far away, you can do the hand signal instead of screaming.

Develop a great "stay" cue/command

"Stay" is a very wonderful command. Your dog can learn to *love* to stay, especially if wonderful rewards come for the behavior of staying. "Stay" means your dog stays, and you move. A dog with a great "stay" command usually has a great recall as well.

Solution

Build a great "stay" command. First, put your dog on a "sit" and say, "Stay," with the five-finger spread hand signal (your dog should see the palm of your hand extended with fingers spread at the end of a straight arm). Simply take one step back, and immediately return to your dog to give a treat. Repeat. Just start with one small step, and continue to reward. Step away from your dog again, and return to give a treat. Your dog is now on a "sit, stay." Return to him a few times, rewarding each time you return to your dog. After two or three treats for the behavior of "stay," release him with an "okay." No treats for the release—only give treats for the behavior being learned. You want to build his drive to want to "stay," instead of a drive to be released. My dogs' stay commands are so strong that I sometimes literally have to pull them up from a stay in the beginning.

Gradually build up to two, three, four, and then many steps away. In the beginning, your hand signal should stay up, so when your dog looks at you, he is reminded to "stay" because he sees the hand signal. Do not say, "Stay," more than once. If your dog breaks the "stay," simply grab the leash, bring him back to the exact spot that he moved from, and then you may tell him, "Stay," again. If he gets up again, bring him back again. Do not give another treat if he breaks a stay. He must stay, even for one second, and wait for his release. Make the "stay" practice short enough for your dog to be successful. In the beginning, it's not about how long he can stay or how far away you can move from him. Simply build a strong "stay" command in close range, then begin to add distance and distraction.

A strong "stay" command can stop a dog in his tracks, which could save his life. In competitive obedience, we have our dogs drop down and stay during a recall. You can work up to this. Make a circle around your dog while he's in the sit position. Have the leash on to prevent a game of chase. If your dog learns that "stay" can mean a potential game of chase, you're doomed. Never chase your dog if he breaks a "stay." With leash on, tell your dog to sit. Hold the leash straight up from the dog's neck with very slight pressure, and show him the hand signal for "stay." Walk a very small circle around your dog, looking at your dog through your hand signal. He should, at this point, be able to see your hand and focus on it the whole way around. When you complete the circle, voice mark, say, "Good stay," and give a yummy treat. Then, you must release the dog from the stay with the word "okay." If your dog does not let you complete the circle, put him back in the exact spot he moved from, face him the same way, and repeat, "Stay." No treat. This can be a slow learning process, but believe me, your dog wants his reward. As soon as he figures out that "stay" means that you can move but he can't, the concept is realized. Once he consistently lets you make a circle, then you can begin to move away into a larger circle.

This exercise should be done on a retractable leash, which adds an extra challenge because it actually pulls the dog toward you, and he has to learn to resist the pressure of the leash. I love teaching "stay" on the retractable leash. It actually takes advantage of the dog's natural "opposition reflex."

You may also use a straight line. Put your pup on a "sit," and tell him, "Stay," as you back away, looking at the dog's eyes through your hand signal. Take two or three steps away—that's it. Voice mark when you're away from him, return all the way back to your staying dog, and give him his yummy treat. Say, "Stay," and back away again, maybe taking four steps this time. Voice mark when you're four steps away, return, and give a treat for the behavior of stay. A very common mistake with stay is to give the reward for releasing the dog, instead of giving the dog his reward while he is still in the stay position. Never give a treat for releasing your dog. All rewards come for the behavior of "stay," which are given to the dog while he's on the stay command. Be very specific with what behavior you are rewarding. If you reward him for being released, you'll create a dog who can't wait to be released and anticipates and breaks his stay because he knows this is when the reward comes. The goal is to create an "I love to be on a stay" type of relaxed attitude. As always, slowly begin to add distractions once your dog understands good "stay" behavior.

Crate training

It's a big mistake not to use a crate with your pup, especially in the beginning. Crates are wonderful for puppies and even for grown dogs with behavioral problems. Crates are an extremely powerful tool for potty training and preventing destructive behaviors when you're out of the home. And you never know when your dog will have to travel in one. It's best to teach your pup to love his crate, and there's a way to do this.

Solution

Crate train. Make sure your dog's kennel is large enough for him to stand up and turn around in. If it's being used for potty training, you do not want it any larger than that. Acclimate him to the kennel so that he likes it and sees it as a safe, happy place before you ever shut the door.

For the first few days, I like to leave the crate door open or even take it off completely. I call this the acclimation period. It may last anywhere from one to three days. Some dogs learn to love their crates right away.

I begin by taking my motivated dog over to the kennel. I throw a yummy treat inside as I say, "Go to your house." He runs in to get the treat and I say, "Yes," as he eats it. He may come back out if he wishes. Then, I keep putting yummy things in there. I may give him a few meals inside the crate, and I'll throw his ball or toy inside and have him run in after it for a fun game. Again, the crate door is open during this period.

As soon as he willingly goes into his crate when you say, "In your house," you may begin to close the door of the crate. If he's quiet for two minutes, open the door and let him out. This teaches him that when he settles down, chews a bone, and relaxes, he'll be let out of his crate. Gradually increase the time he can be in the crate while you are at home before you leave him. If you leave every time you put him in the crate, he'll associate the crate with you leaving, which could create anxiety. When you are home, build up to a good twenty minutes in the crate without your dog panicking. If he can handle this, then you may leave him in his crate.

Be sure to walk him and make sure he's "empty" before leaving him for the first time. It also really helps to have him tired when you leave him, especially the first week or so. Eventually, your dog will actually prefer his crate to den in when you're gone. I also like my dog to be able to stretch out his legs when he sleeps in the crate. A crate resembles what your dog would choose to sleep in in the wild. They love safe, den-like spaces. If you don't provide one for them, they usually end up picking an area in the house that is crate-like.

Unless your dog has to pee or poo, don't let him out of the crate for barking at you, crying, or panicking. Let him out when he's calm and relaxed, and you'll reinforce that behavior instead. Never punish your dog by putting him in the crate. The crate should remain a good, wonderful place for your pup.

Crates are great for dogs with separation anxiety. Let's say you leave, and your dog tears the house apart because he's looking for you. He scratches at the door, howls, and destroys your bedspread and all of your pillows. You then come home in the middle of this chaos. Your dog has just been reinforced for having torn everything up. He thinks his destructive behavior made you come home. When you leave him in a crate, he learns to sleep and chew proper chew toys and that you will eventually come home if he remains calm. I've seen the crate change people's lives. Do it. Always give yummy and proper chew toys to a crated dog. He'll learn to see it for what it is: a safe and relaxing place.

Everything in its right place

I rang the doorbell at Charlie the labrodoodle's house. The owner had called me because Charlie would not "let" anyone through the front door. I rang the doorbell (she had put Charlie in the backyard so I wouldn't be killed), and there, near the front door, was a huge basket of balls, toys, and bones. The owner placed it there along with the leashes because it was easy to grab the leashes and a toy on the way out. Charlie's bed was also in the front room. The toy basket, paired with the excitement of the front door, meant that someone may take his bones and toys. In fact, everyone that walked in was a direct threat to Charlie and his precious toy basket.

I had the owner move the toy basket and put her dog on a leash, and I came to the door again. Charlie let me in. It's not always this simple to correct, but proper placement of food bowls, toy baskets, and crates is important.

Solution

Be conscious of where you place your pup's crate, food bowl, and toy basket. At night, your pup's crate should be in your bedroom so he can den with you. Dog families sleep in the same room. During the day, move the crate to a common area or the area where he can see you. He'll be happier. When you're gone, put the crate in a common room that's used a lot. It should be an open room, *not* a bathroom or a closed bedroom. That will frustrate the dog. It's nice if he can see out a window, as well. But never leave the crate where it can get direct sunlight and heat up during the day when you are gone.

It's best to keep the toy basket up high, so *you* control the toys, not your dog. You can leave a few toys down, but rotate them every day to keep things exciting. Remember, it's very powerful when you control the resources. If you like having the basket on the ground, it should be as far away from the front door as possible. Maybe even put it back in the corner of your bedroom.

Food bowls are good in the kitchen. A lot of bites happen around the food bowls. Definitely do not keep food bowls near the front door. Put food bowls where there is less traffic so the dog can eat in peace and not feel threatened or rushed. If you have young children, it's crucial not to leave food bowls down all day. This is just asking for an accident. Leaving the food bowl down can also cause the dog to "guard" his food. Don't give him the chance to become a picky eater who guards his food dish. Pick up the food after twenty minutes. Feed again at the next meal. If he didn't eat, then he wasn't hungry. It's as simple as that.

Think about these things. By placing the crate, food bowls, and toys in the proper place, you'll have a happier dog.

Establish boundaries

It's very important to teach boundaries to children and dogs. One big boundary is the front door. It's really a pain to have to hold your dog back every time you open the door. Beside that, it's dangerous. He can run toward an unfriendly dog or person or even get hit by a car. There are several other boundaries your dog should learn as well.

Solution

Teach boundaries. Always go through the front door ahead of your dog. Release your pup through the door by saying the word "okay." He's *never* allowed through the door unless you tell him, "Okay." At first, have a leash on your pup. Open the front door. He'll bolt right out. Perfect. Because he's on a leash, he'll either hit the end of it, or you can gently pull him back inside. Close the door and try again. After a few attempts, the dog usually looks up at you instead of running directly out the door. This is when you tell him, "Okay," and let him go through the boundary. He learns that by *not* going out the door, he can get released out the door. Practice until the boundary becomes automatic for your dog, and he can even do it off leash.

Just because you do boundary training does not mean he'll obey the boundary when a distraction is present. When your dog is consistently respecting the boundary 80% of the time in preliminary boundary training, you may slowly add distractions. Set him up. Have a friend wait out front with a friendly dog, maybe even a dog that your dog likes and knows. Open the door with your pup on his leash. If he bolts out, he'll hit the end of the leash, at which point you bring him back in gently, close the door, and try again. He just lost his opportunity to greet his friend by bolting out the door. This is reward removal, because the dog views the friend as the reward. He'll soon learn that if he stops and waits at the door, he'll be "released" with the word "okay" into the fun world. Eventually, the boundary is learned and respected.

Remember, in the beginning he must be on the leash in order to learn. Voice mark and treat your pup for *not* running out the door. This means that the treat comes only for your dog being inside the threshold with the door open. When he willingly waits for a treat, as an added reward, release him with an "okay," and visit the dog and owner that you placed in your front yard. In the dog's mind, he thinks, "Oh, I get it…if I wait at the boundary, I get a treat, and I also get to greet the other dog. If I bolt out, it never works. Mom always brings me back in and closes the door." Keep at it. This could save your dog's life.

Teach your dog how to swim

Dogs, like children, drown every year in swimming pools. I have clients tell me, "Oh, Muffin would never go near the pool. I'm not worried about him drowning." Well, it's precisely these dogs who end up drowning. Your dog can accidentally back up into the pool or fall in while drinking, chasing prey, or playing with another dog.

Solution

Teach your dog how to swim—and how to find the pool stairs. It can save his life. All dogs can learn to swim. I've had chows, pugs, and greyhounds learn to love to swim. It's easy and fun to teach a puppy to swim. An adult dog can be a little more fearful, so get him extra motivated and *hot*.

Your dog should love this game on a hot day. Put on your bathing suit. Get some of your most valuable, yummy treats in a baggie. Get the leash on your pup, and carry him to the first stair in the pool. Immediately begin voice marking and treating your dog for standing on the first stair. You are now teaching him that there is a safe place he can be in the water and still stand up. He should really enjoy standing on the first stair, eating all the yummy treats before you move on to the next level.

When he's relaxed about it, go to the next level, moving his hind legs off the first stair. He may be able to reach the second stair, and maybe not. This is where he learns to hoist himself up onto the first stair for a treat.

Next, carry him out into the water with you. Let go of your dog, and swim as quickly as you can toward the first stair *holding the leash*. By holding the leash, it helps to bring the dog's body into a horizontal position, which is necessary for swimming. Without the leash, he'll panic and begin to swim up toward the sky. This is how dogs eventually drown. The leash needs to gently guide the dog to the first stair, where you always voice mark and treat. Now he's being rewarded for swimming to the first stair.

Try putting him in the pool gently (never throwing him in) from all around the edges of the pool. He should want to swim toward the safety of the first step. Reward him when he gets to the first step. The leash should still be on your dog *at all times* during this training exercise. You should always be holding the end of the leash.

You can even try placing him in the water in the deep end. Put him in the deep end, and walk along the side of the pool as he swims, gently guiding him to the stairs and teaching him how to get out. A dog can drown when doesn't understand where the stairs are, even if he's a *great* swimmer. If he swims to the edge of the pool, he'll exhaust himself because he can't hoist himself out from the side like you can. The goal is to teach him always to swim to the steps. If he swims to the side (which he should not do because you've rewarded him so much for swimming to the steps), you need to tell him, "No," and gently pull him with the leash toward the steps. When he arrives at the steps, voice mark and treat, and allow him to come out of the pool if he wishes (many dogs I train would rather stay in the pool and receive treats).

Now you can have swimming be part of your dog's exercise regimen. See if he'll fetch a ball in the pool and bring it back to the steps for you to throw again.

Your dog should chase you...not the other way around

I see this all the time—chasing your dog. It virtually ruins dogs. For example, I've seen people calling their dog's name as they are running madly toward their dog. This will only push and drive your dog away from you. He thinks you're chasing him and playing, so he'll most likely begin to run from you, creating a wonderful, rewarding game of chase. Or he'll think he's in trouble, and again, he'll move away from you. This also creates a dog who "darts" away when you try and grab his collar. You are teaching him that "come" means you are going to come to him, when it should be the other way around.

The worst thing to do is chase your dog when he steals your favorite pair of shoes or underwear. It's worth letting him eat one pair of shoes, believe me. Do not chase your dog if he steals your valuable items. As soon as you begin to chase him, you are rewarding your dog with a game of chase. Now he not only has your divine shoes or underwear in his mouth, he also gets a fabulous game of chase. He is sure to steal your valuables again. He's faster than you, period, so do not chase him.

Solution

Never chase your dog. It's as simple as that. He should chase you. (The exception, of course, is if he's being injured or is in grave danger.)

Instead, when you want him to "come" to you, run madly in the *opposite* direction. This will get him to chase you instead. As you're running away from him, you should also sound really fun, squeaky, and happy. So what if everyone in the dog park thinks you're nuts. You'll have an excellent dog. He will also think the "come" cue means he gets to chase you, which he'll love, and it's more likely to work when you really need him. (Note: you should formally train your "come" cue as well.)

The other solution: put your shoes away and give proper chew toys. How does he know the difference between your shoes and his toy? Make it easy for him by picking up your mess and leaving his toys on the ground or in a basket. As always, prevention is key.

HUMAN IMPLICATION

What about the guy or gal you're madly in love with? Better *not* chase him. Especially after only seeing him or her twice. You will only drive them away. A call here and there is just dandy, but texting, emailing, and calling all day is sure to bug the person and drive him away from you. It's the oldest rule in the book. Chasing a person or a dog actually drives them away. Be honest, and tell the person you really like him, but don't pester him. Let him be. Let people— and dogs—choose *you*.

Don't discipline the growl…prevent it!

The growl is your dog's warning that something is wrong, and he's about to bite. Don't discipline the growl. When you do, you teach him not to show a warning, and you'll end up with an unpredictable biter who never warns before he bites.

Ever heard someone say, "My dog is so unpredictable, he'll just bite or attack for no reason, with no warning at all?" That's usually a dog who has been punished or corrected for growling. Eventually the growl will go away, and there's no warning for the bite that follows. Don't take away your dog's growl.

Solution

Figure out what's provoking your dog's growl, and work to use prevention and train alternative behaviors. For example, say your dog growls when you try to push him in his cage. If you discipline him, he will hate going into his cage even more. Teach "go to your house," and throw yummy treats inside the crate, instead of physically manipulating the dog into the crate.

Now, let's say your dog is growling at another dog. Instead of telling him, "No," and yanking a choke chain, teach him "sit" and "stay" with voice marking and treating. If he's concentrating on "sit" or "stay," he can't growl. Now, instead of growling and focusing on other dogs, you've shifted your dog's focus to you and getting some yummy treats. You've also changed his motivation by creating a dog who'd rather "sit" and "stay" than growl at another dog.

Eventually, you'll have to deal with potential aggression toward other dogs, but do not take away or discipline your dog's growl. This will only get you one unpredictable dog. You'll probably need to work with a trainer or behaviorist to deal with potential aggression issues.

THE YIELD GAME

Try taking a walk with a friend and one of his or her dogs on a leash. When you yield together and walk in the same direction, you are behaving like a family group, rather than coming face to face with another dog or leering at another dog across the street. Nose-to-nose meetings are unnatural and stressful for dogs. Dogs meet by yielding and merging together. Walk as close as you can, and try to keep your dog's focus on you with voice marking and treating for each time he looks at you. Take a nice walk in the same direction with the unfamiliar dog. This is a great game if you are unsure about the dog you are meeting.

You protect your dog—he should not protect you

A dog is a great deterrent to potential robbers; however, there is no way for your dog to distinguish between a friend and an enemy. If you allow aggression, protection, and territory guarding from your dog, then he's at risk to bite one of your friends, your friends' children, or even the pool man or the gardener. If you leave any dog in the yard by himself, this could happen.

Also, when your dog sits at the window all day and barks at people and other dogs walking by, he's actually practicing a very bad behavior all day long—and he's being rewarded for it, because the people walking by keep going. Your dog believes that he drove them away. This creates a dog who lunges, growls, and begins to show aggressive behaviors when you're out in the world. He's simply been trained to do this at your window all day long. You need to prevent him from practicing.

Solution

Proper socialization is key to creating a friendly dog. From the time he's a puppy, he should learn that people coming into your home are friends. Put a treat in the hands of every person that enters your home, and have your puppy or dog "go say hello" and take the treat. This way, instead of "guarding" his home or you, he can look forward to eating a cookie and not eating your visitors. "Go say hello" is a great exercise to teach young pups to prevent aggression toward people entering your home. It works well for older dogs who are not aggressive as well. If the territoriality over you or your home has begun already, you will need to see a professional trainer.

Don't leave your dog unattended in the yard if you know a worker, employee, or anyone else is coming over to your house. The reason this is so important is because your dog does *not* know the difference between a friend and an enemy. You expect him to be friendly toward your friends, but you want him to attack a robber. Don't leave him alone in the yard, letting him decide who he likes and who he doesn't. This will create a very scary and unpredictable dog.

The first time your dog barks at the gardener or pool man and the worker shows fear or leaves, this reinforces your dog's "protection" instinct. He'll surely do the same—or worse—the next time. You are risking a lawsuit and an unpredictable dog. This all can be prevented. If your dog sits at a window and "practices" bad behavior all day, you need to prevent him from being at that window at all costs. Instead, use a crate with yummy chew bones in it, and take him out on more walks.

Your dog is not there to protect you; you should be protecting your dog. Besides, just having a dog is a sufficient deterrent to robbers.

Recognizing play

Okay, scaredy-pants…relax. Your dog is probably playing. It's important to recognize what fair play is. Some dogs are extremely vocal when they play. Madly barking, play growling, posturing, play biting, grabbing another dog's face with his teeth, and pinching a little—all can be play. You'll even see rolling over and the reversal of roles; really great play mimics a real fight. This is how dogs practice for the real thing, and it's a very important part of your dog's socialization and life to play with other dogs. Sometimes it can look like a real fight, but a trained eye is able to tell the difference.

Play is extremely important for the brain of a younger dog and to sustain a healthy adult. My fourteen-year-old chow mix Eugene still plays. If you constantly worry and think your dog is being aggressive when he isn't, you will eventually cause him stress and anxiety. I see people pulling their dogs out of play all the time. Remember to look at *both* dogs. Look closely at the interaction between the two. Is it mutual? Are they taking turns being the "chaser" and the "runner?" Are there any play bows? Those are all great signs of play.

Your dog will become frustrated if he never really gets to play because you always pull him away from the other dog in a nervous manner. The moment you actually pull your dog away is the most dangerous moment. You are leaving him vulnerable—he's totally incapacitated when you're restraining him—and it frustrates him. Now that he's all wound up and you drag him away from his friend, you could see excitement and play turn into aggression. He'll also always think you're about to pull him out of play, and he'll start to anticipate this—and then it really could escalate into a more tense form of play or change to aggression.

Dogs need to engage in play with one another. Dog play does not always look nice and friendly to the untrained eye.

Solution

Let your pup play. Work with a trainer so you can better understand dog play vs. aggression, and read the dog's body language. Don't get in the habit of pulling your dog out of play. You can actually create an aggressive dog by never allowing him proper play.

And yes, rough play is okay. Take a look at the *other* dog. His behavior will tell you if your dog is playing or not. Is he coming back at your dog? Is he making a play-bow position? These are all signs that the other dog is playing and receiving play signals from your dog. If you hear a loud yelp that resembles a scream or a cry, then it's too rough, and you may separate the play. If one of the dogs is cowering, hiding, and trying to escape, then that is also too rough. The dog will tell you, but you need to be able to recognize when it's not play and when it's healthy play. Aggression occurs when a dog injures another dog and causes harm by puncturing or breaking the skin. If this is happening, you need to get behavioral help. But if he's just playing rough, let it go.

If you have a small dog and you're afraid he'll get hurt, play with dogs that are smaller, but allow your dog to play. This is some of the greatest exercise and fun your dog will ever have. My tiny bichon plays with giant schnauzers, great danes, and pit bulls. In fact, he's usually the boss over the bigger dogs.

"Trying" is not good enough

If you reward a dog for trying, you'll get a dog who "tries," rather than a dog who does the requested command. Once your dog knows "sit," he must sit—not sit with his butt off the ground. "Oh, he's trying!" owners will say and give the dog a treat. Don't do that. Owners also say, "Jack, sit," and the dog does not even approximate sit, and they give the treat anyway. That is precisely how you'd teach him *not* to sit—by commanding "sit" and then treating for not sitting. To the dog, "sit" would mean to stand.

Solution

Be consistent, and only reward for the full correct behavior. Exception: in the *very* beginning, it's okay to reward a couple of close approximations. But know when to move on. You must get more of the correct behavior each time.

Don't be afraid of your dog

If you're afraid of your dog, he *knows* it. This can be dangerous. I highly recommend working with a trainer if you are afraid of your dog in any way.

Imagine the following scenario: you have an eight-week-old puppy with razor-sharp teeth. The puppy can't possibly be aggressive at this age. However, if you squeal and withdraw your hands when he begins to "puppy bite," you've begun to teach the dog that he has power to scare you. He's just learned from you that he can get a fear reaction out of you by using his mouth to bite you. Also, your squeals make you seem like real prey, which excites and rewards the puppy even more.

Kids can really mess up a puppy because they run away and scream when the dog "play attacks" them. This dog will surely get more serious about his job as time goes on. He's also learning that he can chase the children, which could eventually lead to knocking them over or "ankle biting." This will become one of his most favorite games.

All puppies bite, but how you *react* to the puppy is what creates the personality of the dog.

Solution

Prevent fear reactions to your dog, and get help if you are afraid of your dog in any way. Wear leather gloves if you can't stop showing fear reactions. Always equip yourself with a fleece, rope, or other rag-type tug toy when you have a puppy. I always have something in my pocket to help prevent the puppy from chewing on me or my clothes. If you have a toy or a bone, the puppy most certainly will choose the toy over your flesh.

Sometimes, however, he won't; he'll insist on biting your flesh. Be sure to use the early consequence of separation. I stand up, turn away from the pup, and completely disengage. One of my clients has a border collie named Choo Choo. Well, Choo Choo is an exceptional dog, but he developed a very bad habit: he would herd the children in the yard. The kids were so scared that they'd run away and scream, giving Choo Choo some really animated sheep-children to herd around. Everyone thought it was cute and funny, until Choo Choo took his herding job too seriously and sunk his teeth into little Jimmy's leg. Choo Choo the family dog is capable of an aggressive act. It does not mean he's an "aggressive" dog, but he was constantly being rewarded for chasing and herding. Who's fault was it, really? Probably the parents'—the dog's human parents—for failing to realize the ensuing danger that was being reinforced.

If you have a choice, parents with young children should avoid having a herding breed. In the case of Choo Choo, the kids were afraid of the dog…imagine when the owners are afraid of their dog.

Chapter  10

Obedience as a Game

If all the world's a stage, then all of dog training is a game

Think of all training as a game. If cues, commands, and wanted behaviors are games and fun, the dog is more likely to choose to listen. Either you make training fun, or you make it a drag. Your training attitude can create the dog you want.

Cultivate attention

Attention in a dog must be trained. Let's face it—all dogs have ADD. They have very short attention spans, and most people demand way too much of their dogs in the beginning. Attention needs to be built, rewarded, and slowly increased over time.

Solution

Build and reward attention. Cue your dog to "sit." Now, lift your hand signal to your face to create a direct line of eye contact. Voice mark and reward four or five times in a row for sustained eye contact. Then, release your dog with an "okay." Gradually build the amount of time your dog will sustain eye contact using rewards. Remember, if you yell at your dog or sound harsh, he'll avert his gaze. Stay positive with your voice, and slowly build attention during other commands. Pretty soon, your dog will maintain eye contact with you during all commands, until he's "released" with an "okay" into the free world.

Overtraining

Don't ruin training by waiting until your dog quits on you. If you train until he's uninterested, not hungry anymore, or bored, you've over-trained.

Solution

Use short, motivated training sessions a few times a day, and stop training *before* your dog wants to stop. I like to train for five minutes, three to five times per day. Gradually, your dog will have more and more of an attention span if you work with proper motivation. Your dog should look forward to training, and it can be one of the most fun things in your dog's day. My dog will work for six hours. He's a certified Search and Rescue (SAR) dog, and he's actually searched for six hours straight with water and rest breaks. We started with ten seconds and built up to six hours. Go slow and keep it fun.

"Come" is a game

When a dog will not come to you, it's a reflection of many other things going on: either you've never taught him to come, you've never worked with distractions, or you haven't really developed trust, respect, and a bond with your dog. Or, you've poisoned the command.

The come command is the most ruined command in the dog world. I get calls from clients who say, "I don't care about the 'sit,' 'down,' 'stay,' boundary training, or tricks. I just want my dog to *come* when I call him." And that right there is the problem: you have no bond or relationship with your dog. He needs all of the other commands. They all reinforce each other and, in fact, dogs who have a perfect "stay" command usually have an excellent "come" command.

Solution

"Come," more than any cue or command, should be a game, and nothing but a game. The come command should always represent fun. It should be something the dog chooses and wants to do more than anything in the world. How do you achieve this? It starts out with understanding that you may never call your dog for something he sees as negative or even anything that's less fun than what he's doing. Never call your dog to come when it's time to come away from other dogs, go in his crate, get his nails cut, take a bath, come inside from the yard so you can leave the house without him, etc. "When *can* we use the come command?" my clients ask. Not yet. First, you must teach it, then practice, add distractions, and make sure the behavior is at least 80% reliable *with* distractions.

First of all, your dog does not understand what "come" means. You may as well be saying "oyster." He does *not* understand, so don't assume that he does. How do you get him to understand? You name the "come" command as he's performing it correctly. A dog should be sprinting madly to you when you call him to "come." If he dawdles over, he doesn't possess enough excitement and drive to eventually win over distractions in the real world.

The following games will add creativity and fun to your training.

GAMES

THE RESTRAINED RECALL

Begin by having soneone hold your dog's collar. Hang a yummy treat in front of the dog's nose, and sprint madly away. This will make him absolutely mad to get to you. Some dogs will squeal, bark, and pull like crazy to try to get to you. You simply just run away. Now call your dog to "come." Have the other person release the dog, and when he gets to you, treat him and do it again. Of course, at first you need to do this in an area that has no distractions, like down a hallway inside a house. It's important for you to be the most exciting thing in the whole world for your dog during this training.

Why do I have people run away? First of all, it activates the dog's most powerful drive, the prey-chase drive. If you are a running squirrel with a liver treat, he is learning to chase you instead of squirrels. Second, understand that when you stand still, you're actually signaling your dog to stand still. So, it's a mistake to stare at your dog and tell him to "come." You must run away. Always? No. Just until the behavior is learned, and then you can run to keep it fun every once in a while. The chase actually serves as reinforcement, and the dog gets a yummy treat as well. Third, when a mother wolf, dog, or wild dog wants her pups to follow, she just moves away. The pups always follow. She does not have a leash or treats (but she does feed the pups). If she wants the pups to "come," she simply moves or runs away from them. I've seen sixteen-week-old pups cross a small river following their mother. She didn't stand there trying to get the pups to jump in the water; she just left. The pups knew they'd be abandoned if they didn't cross the water. Practice in safe areas, just leaving and moving away from your dog. You'll be surprised how your dog will choose to follow.

THE HIDE-AND-SEEK GAME

Next, we add hiding. Just think of a dog's favorite activities: chasing, eating, and finding prey to chase. Hunting is a huge drive for dogs. Now we add the hunting game into the prey-chase game. Have a friend hold your dog by the collar. Run madly away, and pick a hiding place—in a closet, behind a tree or bush, in another room—totally out of view of the dog. His prey drive was activated by your running away, and now he has to "hunt" for you, which activates his next most powerful drive. When he finds you, you can then start to run away and treat when he "catches" you, or simply just treat when he finds you.

ADD A VOCAL CUE

When you start adding a vocal cue for "come" as you are running away, pay close attention to your tone (see Chapter 5 for more on vocal cues and tone). You must pick a "song" and sound the same every single time you call the dog. For example, if you say, "Noodle, come!" for three weeks, and on the fourth week you say, "Come here, Noodle," it won't work. "Come here, Noodle" is very different from "Noodle, come." And the inflection and "song" you sing for the command must be exactly the same, as well.

KEEP THE NAME POSITIVE

Remember, never call your dog to come when it's time to come away from other dogs, go in his crate, get his nails cut, take a bath, go inside so you can leave the house without him, etc. This will teach your pup to associate "come" with negative consequences and will poison the command. When and if you really need to call your dog out of fun, play, or distraction, *do not* call him to "come." Simply just go and get him. Yes, walk toward him, put on the leash, don't say anything, and leave. This will help prevent you from ruining the come command.

THE TOSS-FOOD-THROUGH-LEGS GAME

Here's a game that I love. Get a huge armful of toys or treats. Start with your dog facing you and your legs spread apart. Put a treat at his nose and toss it between your legs, back behind you. Your dog should go through your legs like a tunnel to eat the treat on the other side. When he's out eating the treat, call him to come, using his name and the word "come." For example, "Noodle, come," and then toss another treat between your legs and repeat. Keep him guessing; he should never know when a toy or treat will be tossed. This game is an absolute blast for the dog and really builds a reliable "come" command.

Your dog learns to respect and trust you during training. It's boring for the dog only to learn one thing. When someone is having problems with "come," I check out all other areas of that human/dog combination first. Begin with other simple commands and cues, and develop consistency before attempting "come" again. Sometimes the best way to solve a problem is by cleaning up everything else around it. A good recall is a reflection of your time and energy, and understanding how to train, positively reinforce, and motivate your pup.

Too much too soon

Don't move too quickly through training exercises. I see this all the time. I was once at a client's house, and we were training the pup to "come" for a treat. The dog had just learned "sit" five minutes earlier, and now we'd moved on to "come." The family kept calling the pup to come, and when the pup exuberantly got to the owner, he commanded, "Sit," and the pup got discouraged and walked away. At this stage, the pup expected a treat for the "come," and instead got a "sit" command.

Solution

In the beginning, separate all the commands and cues, and reward for every correct behavior. Don't move on to a more advanced level right away. And don't cue before your dog knows a behavior. That's right, get the behavior first, and then give it a name. Don't assume your dog truly knows a behavior right away.

Be patient. Go slow. Don't have high expectations. Do your part. If your dog seems frustrated, don't push it. Try again later. Change criteria and add distractions gradually. For example, if you want your pup to "come" over a longer distance, take away distractions, then add them back in when he can come farther. Slowly change one thing at a time.

GAME

TRADE FOR A HIGHER VALUE ITEM

This is the most wonderful game, especially if you have children. It teaches your dog to willingly drop high-value bones and even lets you reach into his food bowl while he's eating.

Have you ever had a dog growl at you because he's eating or guarding a bone? As I explained previously, do not discipline him for growling. Instead, teach him that hands reaching in are good by offering him an even higher-value item from your hand as you take his bone. For example, walk toward him with his favorite liver treat, or even a big piece of meat. He will willingly drop the bone to take the meat that your hand offers. Say, "Drop," at the very instant he drops his bone to take the higher-value item. Pick up his dropped bone as he's eating the meat from your hand, and then, immediately give his bone back to him. He doubles his reward by dropping the bone because he gets a liver treat or meat, and he also gets his bone back. This teaches him that hands reaching in are good and usually have an even higher value food item to offer. It also teaches the "drop" command.

Practice for one minute, three times a day for a few weeks. Always have the higher-value item in your hand. Always show him the high-value item first, as you approach him while he's eating a bone. If he doesn't "drop" his bone immediately, walk away, and go on a walk without him. If he drops the bone right away, give him the meat. If he doesn't drop the bone, you may need to consider that the bone was more valuable than the food item you had in your hand, and you'll need to switch it around the next time you play.

I also like letting my dog eat his plain, dry kibble from a bowl, as I approach with chicken or cheese. I reach right down with the cheese and let him eat it from my hand directly over his food bowl. Again, this helps prevent resource guarding, and he learns that hands reaching in at him while he's eating or chewing on a bone are good things, not threats. The dog thinks, "She offers more, higher-value food and always lets me have my bone back. It's really worth it to drop my bone and let someone reach in at me while I'm eating." Understanding this simple game will help teach your dog to "drop," and it also helps to prevent biting from a dog who feels like he needs to guard his food bowl or bones.

Teach "drop" from walk, stand, or run

The "drop down," or "drop on recall," comes from competitive obedience, but I think it's one of the most powerful obedience exercises. You'll have a really excellent dog if you can master this one. Keep in mind, this is a very advanced cue—so don't get frustrated.

Solution

Teach the "drop down" command. First, make sure your dog knows and understands how to go into the down position from a stand. With your dog standing, guide a treat in your hand from his nose to his feet. He should go into somewhat of a bow position. That's good; voice mark and treat for getting the right idea. Next time, wait until he's all the way down.

Practice the "drop down" close up for a few weeks. Then, begin to take it on the move. With your dog on the leash, walk alongside him, turn in toward your dog, and cue the drop. Now he's learning to drop down from a walk. If he doesn't get it, use the "no reward" word, and don't give him a treat. He's not being disobedient; he just doesn't know the cue from a walk yet. Keep in mind, you've just added a major change.

Try again. When you can drop him from a walk, try dropping him as you run. This is really fun. Once you have the run and drop down, put him on a "stay," and walk away. Now try recalling him to you and dropping him down when he's halfway to you. You can have him on a long line with someone holding it at the starting point in case he decides not to drop, which will most certainly be the case the first few times. Keep trying. If you get to this point in your training, a trainer would be happy to come out and work with you and your dog for just this exercise. It is very advanced, but it's a great goal.

Tug-of-war is good

This is the best game invented for man and dog. When played properly, it can be a great source of bonding and joy for you and your dog. It can also serve as a very powerful motivator and reward. My agility dog only wants to play tug as his reward. He would choose to tug over a food treat every time.

Tug-of-war is an interactive game that you play *with* your dog, as opposed to throwing a ball, which is independent of you. The tug toy is dependent on you holding the other end. Fetch is great, but tug is even better. Your dog will see you as lots of fun, and powerful as well. Playing tug correctly creates a more obedient and bonded dog.

Solution

Play tug-of-war properly by knowing how to teach "drop" and "get it."

Tug dynamics

First, you need to get your dog interested in the tug toy and interested in tugging. Part of the fun of "tug" is that the tug toy resembles and acts like real prey. Real prey does not sit still and hang in the dog's face. First rule of tug: always move the toy away from your dog. You may need to drag it along the ground and run away from your dog until he chases you. This activates his prey drive, which is what we want.

I like using a long fleece or rope tug toy. Fleece is good for pups or beginners, and rope toys can be used later in life. Teach your dog that if he chases the toy, it moves like real prey. If he moves toward it, the toy moves away. He'll finally be so excited that he'll bite onto the tug. Perfect. The second rule of tug: regulate the pressure. Only tug as hard as your dog or puppy is tugging; not weaker, not harder—simply mirror his strength and energy.

Dropping the tug toy

Now for the "drop" part. Holding and tugging with one hand, offer a treat with the other hand as you say, "Drop." If he drops the tug for the treat, great job! He now gets the treat, and then he is allowed to have the toy again. Say, "Get it," as he's getting back onto the tug toy. If he doesn't drop, all play ends. Walk out of the room. He just lost his reward—you tugging with him. Eventually, the "drop" is easy. The dog willingly drops for no treat because it means we get to "get it" again. "Get it" (the chasing and biting of the tug toy) is eventually the reward for "drop."

THE "SIT"/"GET IT" GAME

Next, ask your dog to "sit," and then release him with the word "okay," and say, "Get it." Now tug has become a reward for "sit." Try it with the "down" and "come" commands too.

Tug can be one of the most rewarding games you can play with your dog. It tires him out, creates bond, and helps your dog view you as *fun*. Remember, it's important for you to be viewed as fun by your dog. Why? So he'll *choose* to listen, which is the whole point of this book. We do not force or dominate our dogs into listening. Instead, listening becomes the most fun thing my dog does. It can earn him the chance to tug or be "released" out the door, or it brings him a yummy food reward.

The "touch" cue

I *love* having a good "touch" cue. This means the dog must go up and put his nose on any person or object that you tell him to touch. Eventually, at some point in your dog's life, he will show fear or hesitation toward an object or a person. Maybe a rain coat hanging on a fence freaks him out, or simply a person with a large hat and sunglasses. When you don't deal with the fearful moment, the dog gets what he wants by not having to go near the scary object or person, and his fear is ultimately reinforced.

Solution

Teach your pup to "touch." Start by teaching him to touch objects he knows and likes. Take his ball, bring it down near his nose, and say "touch." When he sniffs or touches the ball with his nose, voice mark and treat. Try objects that he's never seen before; he'll be more likely to want to sniff it. But don't train him on objects he's afraid of, or you'll poison the cue. Use things that won't scare him—a cup, a small box, a picture frame. Say, "Touch," as you bring the new object down into the dog's line of sight. When he touches it, voice mark and treat.

Now practice hand targeting. Hold out the palm of your hand and say, "Touch." He may get it right away. If he doesn't sniff your open palm right away, rub some meat or a treat on the palm so he's encouraged to investigate. As soon as he sniffs your palm, voice mark with "touch," and treat. Soon, he'll conceptualize the game and be able to touch other people's palms and even objects he's slightly frightened by.

I love this cue because people often hold out their palms when they meet a new dog. The palm extended out toward the dog becomes a hand signal for your dog to "go touch." It will immediately relax your dog upon greetings. It's really fun to watch a dog who knows "touch" bop someone's palm.

Don't lead your dog away from fearful situations. It reinforces the dog's fear, and it will only get worse. If your dog spooks at a garbage can or loud noise, don't walk away. Deal with it. Even if you sit across the street from the scary thing and offer your dog treats, that is better than just continuing on your way. If the scary object means you'll give the dog treats, it actually changes his association with the scary thing. I've talked about this in earlier chapters. Walking away reinforces his fear, discipline makes his fear worse, and treating him helps him change his fear to a positive association.

At some point in your dog's life, he's certain to be fearful of something. Touch the object yourself, let him see you touch it, and then tell him to "touch." This is a great game, and it can help with a fearful dog. If you are prepared and know what to do, you can create a well-rounded dog who deals with his fears. When fear is not dealt with properly, or even disciplined, it can lead to aggression, fear biting, anxiety, and phobias.

GAME

NOTHING IS FREE

Consequences drive behavior. We work this way, and our dogs work this way. The word consequence refers to what happens immediately following a behavior. This is how behaviors are shaped. If every time I "sit," I get a liver treat, then I'm way more likely to "sit" the next time I'm asked to. If "sit" means nothing, no reward, or even the removal of a potential reward like getting to say hi to another dog, then I never will choose to sit again. I might even try to bolt away from you when you say, "Sit." Think of your own life in these terms, and try to understand your dog's perspective. Why should he do anything unless there is a desirable consequence?

By calling your dog to "come" or telling him to "sit" and having no reward (consequence), you are actually training your dog *not* to come. If you call your dog ten times for no reward, he will not come on the eleventh time. You've just trained him *not* to come to you. When I tell my clients to "ignore" a barking dog, they are taking away an important consequence: attention. At first the barking may get a little worse as the dog tries harder to get your attention, which always worked in the past. But eventually, he realizes that it doesn't work, and it will stop.

Consequences can be wonderful and positive rewards, like chicken or cheese. A consequence can also mean a missed opportunity for chicken or cheese. We call this "no reward" or reward removal (see Chapter 3). If your dog loves his walk, then have him "sit" in order for the walk to happen. This way, the walk serves as a powerful motivator for the dog to want to sit quickly and precisely to earn it. Use real life rewards. Have your dog "down" before you pick up the leash. The leash *is* a reward because it means a walk. Your dog probably already knows this one. The leash excites him because of what happens every time you pick it up. You never tried to train your dog that the leash is "good," but he loves when you pick up that leash because every time you pick the leash up, you go on a walk. If you were to pick up the leash twenty times a day and never take a walk again, soon your dog will ignore you when you pick up the leash. All of dog training is like this. Everything your dog does can have a good consequence or "no consequence." This is simple learning theory, based in science, not magic.

Make toys more valuable

Dogs, like children, *love* toys. But if you leave all the toys down all the time, they become old and lose their value. It's just like the kid who wants a new bike so bad, and then he gets the bike, rides it like crazy for a week or two, and begins to want a different toy. We're all guilty of this.

Solution

Create "valuable toys" by rotating them, and then use them for training. Instead of just throwing toys all over the ground, have a basket of toys up high somewhere in the house. Every day, take three new toys down and put three old ones back in the basket. When they come out again, it's like they are new. Call your dog to "come," and instead of a treat, give him a new (or rotated) toy. If he likes to chase, throw the toy and say, "Get it!" Ask him to "sit." When he sits, throw the toy or run dragging the toy on the ground. This should make him want to bite onto the toy and tug with you. As I mentioned earlier, tug is one of the best games you can play with your pup to have fun and build bond. If "sit" or "come" means you'll throw the ball or hand over a new toy, your dog is more likely to "sit" and "come."

Obedience tips and exercises

Fade the lure/reward

Eventually, you must begin to use intermittent reinforcement. This means that instead of treating *every* time, you now start to vary the rewards. Sometimes you can vary the number of correct responses before a reward, and sometimes you'll vary the length of time between rewards.

Once a behavior is learned, which means the dog will perform correctly 80% of the time, even with distractions, then you may begin to "fade out" the treat. *But not completely.* When the treat goes away, so will the behavior, unless you understand how to fade out the reward properly. Take the "sit" cue. First, make sure it's 80% reliable. Then, you may ask for two "sits" for one treat, and eventually three, and then five "sits" for one treat. Then, you can ask for a "sit," have the dog hold the sit for one minute, then reward. Eventually, he'll hold the sit for two or three minutes, and then you reward.

You can also do a combo: have your dog do a chain of behaviors that he knows, all for one treat instead of a treat for each one. You might have him "sit," "down," "stay," "come," and then "heel" for five minutes before your first treat. Keep it random, and always preserve the potential to win a "jackpot" of treats.

The idea with 80% learned behaviors is to keep it exciting, and always let your dog wonder when he'll receive the reward. This creates a dog who loves trying to earn his yummy reward. Even if he does training on his entire walk, have one treat ready for him at some point during the walk, and he will never know when this moment may be. One day use treats, and the next day, don't use treats. Always have them on you, however, or he'll learn to listen only when you have the treat pouch. I like to ask for a behavior in the living room, and if I get a correct response, I'll run to the kitchen and get out a treat. Sometimes I'll run into the kitchen, and sometimes not. The important part is that there is *always* potential for your dog to earn his reward.

People always want to know when they can stop using treats. I tell them, "When you start going to work every day for free," and they get the point. If you never reward learned behaviors, the behaviors will eventually fade. Would you rather fade the treats? Or the behaviors? Your choice!

Only reward the behavior being learned

Let's say your dog knows "sit" and "down," and now we're trying to teach "roll over." The reward should not be given for the "sit" or "down" parts, but saved for the "roll over." Understand how to raise the criteria gradually. For "roll over," you need to get the dog into a "down" position first. If he keeps getting the reward for the "down," why would he want to "roll over?" The key is to reward successive approximations of the correct new behavior.

For example, maybe the first time you reward for the "down." The second time, the "down" is free (no reward), and you lure the dog with a treat that he really wants, causing him to roll over just a little onto his side. You do this by bringing the treat from your dog's nose to his belly. When he's on his side, give the reward. The dog hasn't done a full "roll over," but he went on his side. Each time you repeat, get closer and closer to the "roll over." Next, he must roll onto his side and then onto his back. He gets a treat. Keep going until you can tease him with the treat *just* enough out of reach for him to "roll over" in order to get it.

The deadly sin to this method is that you can never reward for a *lesser* approximation of the desired new behavior, only a *greater* approximation each time. If you had your dog on his side, and then the next time he only got into a "down" position, then *no reward* is the best choice. If you go back to giving a treat for the "down" when you're trying to get a "roll over," you'll confuse the dog into thinking that "roll over" means "down" because that's the behavior you're rewarding. If you're working on "stay," only reward the stay by returning to your dog and treating while he is still on the "stay" command. Too many times the dog "stays," and then gets his cookie only after being "released" from the stay position. This rewards the "release," not the "stay." And next time, your dog will anticipate the treat by "releasing" himself. You never need to reward the release. Freedom is enough of a reward.

If you are working on "stay," then get a stay. If your dog keeps breaking the "stay," and you put him back on a "sit" and "stay" and give him another treat, he learns to break his stay position because it means a double reward. He thinks, "If I break my 'stay,' I get put back on another 'stay' and get another treat."

Next time, he's sure to break his stay again. Instead, have a continuous flow of treats delivered for the behavior of "stay," and only the behavior of "stay." If he gets up, end the game and go into another room. Or, bring him back, ask for a "stay" on the leash, and then release him for no reward. He "lost" his opportunity to earn a reward because he broke his "stay."

Environmental cues

I love environmental cues. The doorbell can mean "go to your spot;" a person's outstretched palm can mean "go say hello" or "go touch."

Here is a great example. Every day, my dogs would chase Mr. Squirrel outside on the fence. It was usually a five- to ten-minute barking festival, and my dogs loved it. One day, I waited with a box of liver treats. As soon as Mr. Squirrel came, I shook the liver box loudly, squeaked, and called my dogs to come. I began to do this every day, but only when the squirrel came out. Eventually, the squirrel became the cue for my dogs to get a liver treat. Soon, when they saw Mr. Squirrel, the barking stopped and they'd run to the cookie jar and wait for their treat.

I like using the doorbell as an environmental cue for "go to your bed." I place a mat or a dog bed in view of the door, but still a safe distance away. I start by teaching "go to your bed" as I throw a treat onto the bed. Next, I have someone outside. I have the person ring the bell, and I immediately say, "Go to your bed," and throw a treat. Yes, the first few times he'll be all riled up because the bell is ringing. But be patient, and he'll eventually go to his bed. And when he does, it "magically" brings the person inside! He learns that going to his bed actually brings the person in to see him. And the person should have a second treat, which is also given on the dog bed. Eventually, when the dog hears the doorbell, he'll automatically go to his bed. No vocal cue necessary. The doorbell is the environmental cue for "go to your bed." As always, use really high-value rewards, and be patient and consistent when training.

Be creative and come up with other environmental cues. Picking up the leash can mean "sit." Every time you pick up the leash, say, "Sit," and do not continue moving forward for his walk until he "sits" for the leash to be put on. If he dances around, pull the leash away, cross your arms, and walk away. Try again in thirty seconds. If he sits, continue the game by putting on the leash and going on the walk. Pretty soon, picking up the leash becomes your dog's cue to "sit." You won't even have to say it.

Food bowls prepped on the kitchen counter can mean "down." When your dog goes into a "down" position (use a lure at first), put down the food bowl and let him go at it. Be creative. Think of how many environmental cues you can come up with. The sky is the limit.

This way!

I absolutely love teaching dogs the "this way" command. "This way" means "change directions" or "do a 180-degree turn." Why? It's a great way to get your dog to come your way without poisoning your "come" command.

Start with your dog on a leash, and trot out with him. I like starting this game at a walking pace, and quickly moving up to a jog, a run, and even a sprint. Begin by holding the leash and walking silently in one direction. When your dog is moving out with you, pivot and make a 180-degree turn, and say, "This way," in a really animated and exciting voice. When he jogs along with you and changes directions, give a treat or a tug toy. Then, repeat. Get good enough to play this game off of a leash. Always give him something desired when he changes directions with you. If he does not change directions, run inside, close the door, and hide. Your absence works magic—he just lost his chance for a reward.

It's best to play the game first in the boring house, so that you are the most exciting thing around. You must practice "this way" when there are no dogs or distractions around, and then you can gradually begin to add distractions. If "this way" always means there's another dog around, he will probably begin to associate the command with other dogs. When you first decide to work with distractions, be sure your dog is hungry and set it up to have a place to "escape" to where he can't get to you. This is a very important part of the game. He learns that if he does not follow you, he gets left or loses the potential reward. If you're out hiking, change directions for no reason, and say, "This way." When your dog follows, give him a treat and continue the hike. "This way" should never be the end of his freedom or the end of the hike. Do it the whole hike. Now try it around other dogs. If he changes directions with you, treat and let him run back to the other dogs. If he does not change directions with you, hide behind a tree.

Tricks

Teaching tricks is very important—it enhances your dog's vocabulary and creates a fun game that you and your dog can play together. If your dog only knows "sit" and "down," he will get bored after a while. Tricks help remind you (and your dog) that training should and can be a blast. My Aussie used to bring me a beer or a water from the fridge, and he'd also bring my bags to the car for me. Really! I taught my Aussie a new trick every single day of his life. Whether it was teaching the name of a new toy or a physical trick, we never missed a day.

Teaching tricks and words creates a thinking dog who thinks you're really neat and interesting. Why is that important? Because dogs do not and will not listen to boring people. Tricks are *fun*. Here's a few to teach your dog.

TRICKS

♦ Spin: Start with a yummy treat at your dog's nose level. Slowly lure the dog's head back toward his own tail, and then back around to the front again. He should want to spin in a circle. Treat him when he completes the circle.

♦ Shake a paw: Hold some really yummy treats at nose level with your dog in a "sit" position. If he's really interested in the treats, he'll usually "paw" at them. As soon as he "paws" the hand with treats in it, open up your palm, and give him a treat. Next level: when he paws at the hand full of treats, grab his paw gently with the other hand, and immediately follow with a treat.

♦ High Ten: With your dog in a "sit," give him the palm of your hand just above his nose. If you have really yummy treats in your hand, he will lean back and up and place both paws on your hands full of goodies.

♦ Back up: Hold food at nose level, and push gently back on the dog's nose. When he takes a tiny step back, voice mark and reward. Each time get more steps backward before treating. Soon he'll be running backward. Have a good time, and don't give up.

Chapter  11

Energy, Exercise, and Fun

Exercising your dog

You got a Jack Russell terrier and are complaining about him being crazy…. Well, you need to tire him out. Exercise is one of the keys to a healthy, happy dog. No amount of training can "cure" a dog that is just wound up with extra energy. Exercise is good for you, too.

Solution

Exercise your dog. There's so much more you can do than just "walking" your dog. You can bike with your dog, rollerblade, or teach a mean game of fetch. I've even helped several clients "treadmill" train their dogs. Soon, the dog will go over to the treadmill and "ask" for a run. Never use the treadmill in place of a real outdoor excursion. Change things up! Don't do the same old boring routine every day. Go to the beach, take a dog-friendly hike in your area, or meet other dogs for a play date.

The same goes for humans. Every mother knows to put a hyperactive child in sports! Karate, baby…. It just works.

You can also teach your pup how to "go find" around the house and eventually, the yard. Start by taking a bit of cheese, and let him see you place it on the ground. Then say, "Go find," as he sprints to the cheese bit and eats it. Next, have him sit and stay where he can still see you (if he doesn't know sit and stay yet, you can tie him up). Place the bit of cheese farther away, and then around the corner where it's not visible to your dog. Tell him to "go find." I've had clients' dogs searching for an hour at a time to find a hidden cookie. Remember, their noses are extremely powerful. Eventually he will "smell" where the tidbit of food is.

Most dogs need an hour a day of fun exercise. Be sure to find time and a safe place for your dog to have off-leash time with other dogs. This is great for tiring them out. A tired dog is a good dog—and a fulfilled one, as well. It's not fair to discipline bad behavior if it's just a reflection of boredom or lack of exercise and stimulation. Keep in mind, training also counts as "brain exercise" and will tire the dog out in a different way. Use both physical and mental training.

Don't run too far

A dog is made to run and sprint, and then stop. Run and stop. He also likes to do a jog and stop, and then jog some more and stop. To make your dog run with you for twenty minutes or more without stops may be too much for your particular dog or breed. I've even seen people run their dogs for an hour, which is downright abusive. He could easily suffer heat stroke. Your dog can't tell you it's too much or that he wants to stop.

If you do a short run/stop with your dog, he should have water available every five to ten minutes, depending on the heat.

Solution

Go for a jog-walk-jog-walk. A dog should not run for more than five minutes without being able to get water or come to a walking pace. You may think your dog is happily jogging along with you, but remember, his system is different than yours. He feels thirty degrees hotter than you, and dogs can't sweat. The only way for a dog to "sweat" is through his feet or his mouth (by panting). He does not have sweat glands all over his body like you do and can only slightly dissipate heat through panting and through the pads of his feet. There is a very high chance of your dog suffering from heat exhaustion simply because he has no way to sweat.

If you were off-leash running around with your dog and he had his choice, he'd come to a complete stop and rest in the shade every five minutes or so. You need to know and respect this because your dog does not have a voice to tell you.

Let your dog run off leash

Usually, fear keeps people from letting their dogs run free. Not only is he missing out on great exercise and off-leash play with other dogs, which is crucial for development and health, but you're creating a dog that "wants" and "yearns" to escape. When you don't allow him to sprint and run, it's all he'll think about. And then, watch out if you ever drop that leash—you've created a monster. He most certainly will bolt.

Dogs can become aggressive or fearful of other dogs if they never learned how to play properly off leash. The longer you keep your dog from running with other dogs, the more likely he will be to develop fear or aggression issues with other dogs.

Solution

Let your dog run free. All dogs need to play *off* of the leash. Find a *safe*, fenced-in dog park or dog-friendly hike (great options are usually listed around town or online). There are even "dog beaches" in certain areas. Find a friend with a big yard, and have a play date with your dogs. This is great. Off-leash play in the backyard with other dogs is wonderful for your dog. There are great risks to your dog if you never let him play off a leash and run free. He could get extremely hurt because he's out of shape and doesn't understand how to "roll" and bump into other dogs. He'll become overly sensitive to other dogs' play motions and contact.

The key to healthy off-leash play is to start young. Pups learn about their world through play and running with other dogs off leash. You are not a dog, and your dog knows you're not a dog. There are certain things that you can't possibly teach him about other dogs. He must learn those lessons from other well-behaved, friendly dogs. If you start young and put your dog around safe, clean, and friendly dogs, he'll be great. If you're scared or you don't know how your dog will act, it's best to contact a positive-reinforcement trainer or behaviorist to help you determine what is going on. Find a safe way to let your dog run free.

He's been waiting all day

Your dog is happy to see you. He's been alone all day, and no, he did not entertain himself. Dogs do not exercise themselves. Please respect your pet, and he will respect you.

Solution

Engage with your dog when you get home. Take the time to do something *he* likes. Your idea of fun may be watching TV with him, but I assure you he'd rather be out walking or playing with you. Do a short training session first. Remember, when a dog has to think, it also tires him out, which means that you can relax soon.

If you're gone for work for more than eight hours, you may want to think about getting a dog walker to come in the middle of the day, depending on your dog's breed, age, and energy level. I know you're tired when you come home. But if you dedicate a little time to your pup, he'll be fulfilled for the rest of your evening and will let you relax.

Don't be a bore

I had a teacher in ninth grade who managed to make a subject I absolutely loved extremely *boring*. He did this because he had no enthusiasm or energy when he taught. It didn't matter that it was a subject I loved—I would fall asleep and miss everything he said. People get too serious and boring when training their dogs. That's why I hate the word "obedience."

Solution

Be fun! Think of training as teaching your dog *games* instead of thinking of it terms of "obedience." Make everything a fun game. Your dog is like a child. He prefers an animated voice with energy, especially when he's learning from you. If you are the most exciting thing out there—*more* exciting than other dogs or squirrels—your dog will actually come to you when you call him. You need to focus on being fun with your dog, or he'll be distracted and interested in everything but you.

What is fun to your dog? I'll answer for him: squeaky voices, animated voices, movement, running away from him and letting him chase you, playing tug-of-war with you, hiding and having your dog come find you, throwing a ball or a toy and running in the opposite direction, treats, treats, treats, hot dogs, cheese, steak, chicken, fish, lamb, roast beef, turkey, frozen blueberries, marrow bones, and new toys, even if it's just an old rag. Get the picture?

Give your dog a job

Jobs give us something to do, and hopefully they add meaning to our lives. We all love to have a purpose, and when we don't, we're usually looking for one. Work, or "jobs," help us to feel confident and worthy, especially when we love our work.

Solution

Give your dog a job! Dogs are very much like humans in this regard—most should have a job. A job can be life changing for your dog. His job can be as simple as fetching a ball or as advanced as certifying him in Search and Rescue so he can find missing persons. Whatever job you create for your dog, you're certain to see a happier, more relaxed, and fulfilled dog.

A job is different from basic exercise. It usually involves the mind more. Teach your dog to "find" a cookie or a ball, as previously discussed. Name toys and treat him for "touching" or bringing you the correct toy. You can be really creative with this. What is your dog's job? Remember, dogs were bred to be working dogs. Even the lap dog takes great pride in keeping your lap warm.

Keep in mind, if you don't have a job for your dog, he'll find one of his own, and you may not like what he comes up with: barking, digging, running away, stealing shoes….

When to baby your dog

There is a time to be supportive and give your dog the love he needs, but babying your dog all day long does him no service. I see this with lap dogs a lot. For some reason, people carry their little dogs around like babies. The dog wants to walk! A dog who is babied in your arms is often snappy and aggressive with other people who try to reach out and pet him. Dogs that are carried all day lack proper socialization. Do not baby-talk him when he's growling at another dog or person, saying, "Oh, sweet baby. Don't growl, honey. It's okay, boo boo bear!"

Solution

Have a time and place for babying. It can be fun sometimes, just not all the time. Create a fun, energetic, and motivating voice for your dog, and let him be a dog. He's not going to be killed by a wild animal or another dog if you're supervising him in a safe place. Don't be afraid, or you'll create a dog who's afraid. And remember, fear often leads to aggression.

If you're overprotective with a dog or child, he'll lack proper socialization, and eventually, he'll rebel. Your tiny, baby Chihuahua longs to run with other dogs. Dogs need to get dirty, dig in the sand, run like a wild maniacs, and play frantically with you and other dogs. He's *not* an infant; he's a dog. Behavioral problems can develop when you treat him like a baby. Remember, late at night, or when you're relaxing by the TV, it's great to talk quietly and lovingly to your dog. You can even baby him in those moments, and he'll love it. But if you do it all the time it loses its value, and you will surely irritate your dog.

Proper chew toys

Stuffed toys, soft toys, and plastic toys are not enough. Proper chew toys give your pup something to do. A great chew is good for his teeth and can help keep them clean. Chewing something also expends energy and can help tire your dog out.

Solution

Give your dog proper chew toys. Soft, plastic, and nylon toys are okay, but they usually won't really satisfy your pup's chewing or teething needs. A dog needs to chew when he's teething, but also, dogs love to chew on bones and other objects their whole lives. When you leave him in his crate, always give him a chew.

Chewing gives dogs great pleasure. They should be able to have chews available all the time. I love giving my dogs bully sticks and braided bully sticks. These are very hardened, tendon-like chews. They last a long time, they're fully edible, and dogs love them. Cow hooves are also very hard and last a long time. And they're cheap!

I also like giving my dog real, raw marrowbones or knuckle bones in his kennel. You can get them from your butcher—they are very inexpensive. Have him disc the marrowbone into hockey puck–like shapes. Freeze and give them to your dog raw and frozen. This way, it takes him twice as long to get out the yummy marrow. For a teething puppy that can have sore gums, the cold from the frozen bone helps with the pain from teething. I sometimes wet a rag, freeze it, and let the pup chew on that. The Kong Toy is virtually indestructible and safe. It has a hole in the center that you can stuff with cheese, peanut butter, or even wet dog food. I also freeze this one so it takes the dog longer to get out the yumminess.

If you don't have proper chew toys, your dog will chew your house apart. Dogs especially love wood, so be careful to teach him what's his to chew by placing proper chews in his crate. If you see him chewing or showing interest in wood or chair legs, gently pull him away, and replace with a proper chew. If a dog has a choice between a marrowbone or a shoe, I promise you he'll choose the marrowbone. If there are no chews around, he'll most definitely choose your shoe…hopefully not the Gucci loafers.

Remember to rotate chews each day so they stay interesting and new to the dog. Don't throw all the toys and chews down at the same time.

PROPER CHEWS

♦ Bully sticks (braided or tube shaped)
♦ Cow hooves
♦ Raw marrowbones from the butcher (feed frozen and raw)
♦ Marrowbones form the pet store—stuff them with yummy filling such as peanut butter, cheese, chicken, wet dog food, etc., and freeze (frozen goodies take twice as long to eat!)
♦ Kong toy stuffed with something soft, frozen, and yummy

Chapter  12

Potty Training

Potty train your pup!

To begin, don't leave food out all day. Learn your dog's schedule, and time your potty training with when he has to go.

With potty training, prevention is key. Dogs like to pee where they've peed before. Once he starts peeing in the house, it becomes harder and harder to change his spot. In the beginning, take your dog to his proper potty spot until you get a potty. That alone will encourage him to want to go back to that same spot. If he does soil the house, this is usually because he was running free or his crate or kennel is too big and he went to the bathroom in his own house. If this happens (which it shouldn't) clean it up with an enzymatic cleaner, and work on prevention and *reward* for potty in the correct location.

Treat your dog with a food reward at the exact moment that he is peeing. Yes, feed your dog as the pee is coming out. This is proper timing. You can also say, "Go potty," or whatever word you want to use for potty on command. In the beginning, you must time the word and the treat with the action of pee coming out.

When you are home with your pup, you must watch him like a hawk. Tether him to your belt loop, or have him in the crate until he's fully potty trained. Tethering is a great option to use as a potty training tool. Tie him to *you*. After a week or two of bringing him out to potty and rewarding him for going in the proper spot, it's time for him to ask you to be taken out. This will not happen if he's running loose. Keep him on the tether, and *wait*. When he has to go, he will begin to whine, bark, whimper, or paw at your leg. Take any of these as a "signal" that he has to go potty. Immediately respond to the signal by taking him out to his special potty spot, and then, after he potties in his correct spot, reward him by taking your walk. Yes, you can use the walk itself as a reward for potty in the correct spot.

Use the two-minute rule. If he doesn't potty in two minutes, go back inside, and place him in his crate or on his tether. Try to go outside again in ten to fifteen minutes. Stay out for another two minutes, then repeat. When he finally potties, take your walk. If he doesn't potty, he gets tethered or put in his kennel. Remember, the kennel is *not* a punishment; you're simply putting him in there because you know he has to go. This prevents him from having an accident in the house. He'll learn to go right away when you take him out because he "earns" his treat and walk.

POTTY = PARTY!

POTTY MEANS THE WALK BEGINS, NOT ENDS

I like this one because as soon as I tell clients, they have an "ah-ha!" moment. Most people take a walk to try to potty train their puppies. You walk and walk and walk, and the pup is having a great time. Finally, the pup pees and poops, and you immediately turn around and head toward home. The pup learns that every time he goes potty, it means the walk is over and we go home. He loved walking and sniffing and smelling the roses, but as a consequence for potty, the fun ends, and you turn around and go home. This is a negative consequence for pottying, and your dog will learn to hold it and train *you* to take longer walks.

Instead, teach your pup that going potty = a party. Potty means the fun walk *begins*. Have a potty spot in the back or front yard, and don't begin the walk until the pup pees in his spot. Have your pup on leash, and give a voice mark and a treat for going potty in the correct spot. The leash ensures that he won't run around sniffing and having fun until he potties. Don't let your pup run free, even in the backyard, until he potties. Freedom and taking a walk can be used as rewards for going potty. Now your dog thinks, "Oh, I'll have to potty right away so we can go on our walk!" And now you help create a dog who goes out and empties himself right away.

You can do the same thing without going on a walk at all. Take your pup out on a leash. Do *not* walk around; just take three steps back and forth. As soon as he potties, voice mark, treat, and take off the leash. Now, he's free to play in the backyard as a reward. You're sure to create a pup that goes outside and potties right away.

Submissive urination

When your dog pees at your feet when you come home from work, this is called submissive urination. If you discipline him, the problem may get a lot worse.

Solution

You must ignore submissive urination. To help, make your entrances and exits very calm. Try waiting three to five minutes after you get home before making eye contact with your dog or saying hi. Don't come home squeaking and gushing with kisses, scratches, and treats. All the excitement is actually causing him to pee. Instead, when you come home, avoid eye contact and saying hello for a few minutes. I know this is hard, but pour yourself a glass of water, or a cocktail, and *then* say hello in a gentle way. Usually the problem will diminish if you do this. You must tell all your friends to play by the same rules: greet the pup only after a few minutes, and do so calmly.

Use the proper crate

Dogs learn to love their crates when used properly. Crates work for potty training because a dog does not want to soil the area he's hanging out in. Help him by using a crate when you are gone. A dog does not want to pee on himself and then sit in it. So when you use a crate, he will learn to hold his pee, and then he can release himself when you take him out. This gives you a chance to reward him.

When your crate or pen is too large, your puppy will use it as a bathroom. By using a smaller crate, he learns to hold it in, and then you'll have success when you take him out. If your puppy is using his crate or pen as a potty area, make it smaller, and only leave him in there when he's "empty."

Nighttime potty breaks for puppy

Don't leave your puppy in a different room all night so that he won't wake you up if he needs to pee. This can be detrimental to potty training. If you leave your pup in another room all night, you'll miss his cries for "I have to potty," and he'll be forced to soil his crate.

Solution

Let your pup go pee, even if this means getting up in the middle of the night to take him out. A pup is a big commitment, almost like having a baby. You need to be sure you can commit to the time it takes to potty train him. If you don't, he'll end up soiling his crate and will learn to be a dirty dog. Would you want to poo and then sleep in it all night?

Spite pees

This one is my favorite—when you think your dog peed on the carpet just to spite you. If you come home to find that your dog has peed on your bed, he was probably anxious about you being gone, so he went to the area that smelled the most like you. When he got there, he was so wound up that he peed. More often, it's because you have not properly potty trained your pooch.

Solution

Potty train your dog. It will prevent potty accidents in the house. I know you want to believe your dog is mad at you, but really, this is not possible. Please don't blame your dog. Dogs don't hold grudges or do things to punish you. I'm sorry to say it, but this is your fault. Either your dog is not potty trained, or his peeing is a reflection of some sort of anxiety.

Chapter  13

Breed Considerations

The right breed for you

Many people make the mistake of taking on a dog who isn't right for them. In fact, I had an entire TV show on Animal Planet based on this mistake. Time and time again, I see problems that stem from getting a dog that doesn't suit your personality. This happens most often when people get dogs for their image, or because they're "cute."

Just like people, personality varies widely among the breeds and within breeds. If you're a sedentary person, I wouldn't start out trying to find a mellow terrier, vizsla, or Australian shepherd; I'd begin with a large, lumbering breed: St. Bernard, newfoundland, great pyrenees, or maybe a little Japanese chin lapdog. Once you know the general breed that is right for your personality and exercise needs, begin to assess the personality of the dogs within the correct breed for you.

Solution

Do research and be sure you are getting a dog that fits your energy, personality, and exercise level. Talk to people, and spend time at a dog park to see how different dogs act. Spend time at a shelter, and volunteer to take dogs on walks for a few weeks. Go to your shelter with a professional trainer or behaviorist to help match you with the right dog. Don't just pick one because he's cute. They're all cute.

A ten-year-old greyhound may be a great pet. I had one client who was in her seventies. We went and rescued a ten-year-old greyhound—it was the perfect pet for her.

Get a dog for your personality, not for your image. This is more common than you think. The tough guy wants a pit bull, but he may not have the time for an energetic breed. People are drawn to dogs at first because of the way they look and how that dog will make them look. For example, do you ever see a big man with a toy poodle? Not often, yet toy poodles can be a great, athletic, smart dog for a single guy. But it seems like the single guy more often has a bigger dog; a lab, retriever, a rare breed, or a good old mutt.

Understanding your breed will give you lots of information about what your dog needs. At the very least, it will help you to know how much exercise he requires. A herding breed will herd if you don't give him a proper outlet for it. This can be retrieving, or watching his "sheep" (you) from a distance. A good sheepherding dog (a real one) will just watch the sheep and control his impulses for hours. He learns to stay back and watch. It's possible to train a herding breed *not* to herd, but if you're worried about this at all, you should not get a herding breed. He will herd the children if left to his own desires.

Oftentimes the breed that's right for you may not be the one you imagined in your head. Trust me, if you find the one that's right for you, you'll be way happier in the long run. You'll love him so much that he'll be the most beautiful dog in the world to you. And, *all* dogs are chick or dude magnets. I *love* when a big guy has a fluffy little pup!

HUMAN IMPLICATION

Ever chosen the wrong person as your mate? This is where dating services come in. With the dating services, you are at least starting off with common interests, life goals, and moral values. From there, you can see if you have the "spark." Most of my married friends found their spouses online.

This is why "setups" work so well. When people set you up with a friend of theirs, they inherently know that you'd go well together. A random walk down the street is not likely to produce the perfect match. Yet, this is usually how we meet our partners, and our canine friends. We just think they're cute— and this can be very dangerous.

Check yourself…. When you find your heart pounding, and it's love at first woof, step back. There most likely *is* a very good reason you're drawn to that cute little doggie, but be sure it's for the right reasons and that *you* have the time for him. Don't let your kids talk you into a puppy unless you are ready, because I guarantee you, you'll be raising and training the puppy, not the kids.

Every dog is unique

My master trainer used to say that there are more differences within a breed than there are between breeds. You can't assume, for example, that all labs are the same. *Most* labs are happy-go-lucky, friendly, great with children, and trainable. But I've seen labs bite children, attack other dogs, and be aggressive toward people. Although he's a lab, he still has a unique personality. His upbringing, socialization, training, and environment all make a big impact on who he is and how he'll behave as a lab.

Solution

When picking a dog, consider his personality as well as his breed. Breed means a lot, but it doesn't mean *everything*. If you're unsure about a dog's personality, bring along someone who is trained to help you when picking a dog.

There is as much difference within a breed as there are between breeds. Simply stated: I can show you a mellow retriever, a hyper retriever, an aggressive retriever, etc. Knowing your breed gives you an excellent start, but you also need to assess behavior. I've met the anomaly of every breed—friendly pit bulls who are great with children and really aggressive golden retrievers.

Understand that common dog myths are often just not true. For example, small dogs can be more energetic and need more exercise than larger breeds. Greyhounds make great apartment dwellers, and so do Saint Bernards and great danes. These are huge dogs that do really well in apartments with no yard. Pit bulls can be friendly and labs can be aggressive. Hunting breeds can be a handful. Labs and retrievers can be exuberant and have tons of energy, or they can be mellow. Terriers have tons of energy. They were bred to bark and "rat out" vermin from their holes.

MALE VS. FEMALE

If you already have one dog, it's probably best to introduce the opposite sex when bringing home a second pet. This reduces competition and will decrease the chance of aggression. Here are a few generalizations about male and female dogs.

♦ FEMALE DOGS. Females can be easier to train, tend to be more passive, can be more affectionate, and make better companions. (Note: these are generalizations; I've always had super affectionate male dogs). Females can hold urine longer than males, and females empty their bladder all at once instead of marking (although some females do mark).

♦ MALE DOGS. Males make better watch dogs and are generally more self-confident. And males are less expensive to neuter than females are to spay.

Replacing a Pet

This happens a lot. You had Buddy, the *best* dog in the world. Buddy was a German shepherd. Buddy passes on. What tends to happen a lot is that people want to "replace" the pet by getting another German shepherd. But the new German shepherd will probably never live up to Buddy's status and charm. I suggest trying a different breed altogether. Not only is it very rare to get a dog with the same personality as the one you had before, but every time you look at your new shepherd, you'll see Buddy. Not that it's a bad thing, but the new dog can never really replace or live up to your old pet.

Try a different breed or mixed breed. There's so much to learn from different breeds and personalities.

Acknowledgments

There are so many people in my life who've inspired me and given me the passion and energy to move forward in living my dream. Thank you to my love Gerald Minniti, who has been my support through this whole process. Thank you to Max and Evan Minniti, who reminded me how special my own dogs are. Thank you to Richard Vye, who trained me to train dogs, and changed my life.

Thank you Michael Broussard, who saw the talent, inspiration, and believed in me from the very beginning. Thank you to everyone at Phoenix Books: Dan Smetanka, Gray Peterson, Ryan Quinn, and Kimberly Miletta. Ryan, thank you for all the great editing sessions!

Thank you to Jim Knowles and Gerald Minniti for photos. Thank you Mom and Dad, for always allowing me to express my passion in animals. Thank you to all of my dog-training clients, for believing in me, and living the advice. Thank you to all the positive reinforcement trainers who have been an inspiration for me: Ian Dunbar and Karen Pryor. Thank you Animal Planet, and thank you, Bonnie Hunt!

Thank you to the Association of Professional Dog Trainers, for sharing the knowledge of the science behind dog training, and echoing the voice for positive reinforcement training throughout the world. Thank you to my Uncle Gene Zaphiris and Matt Stander for exposing me to a world of dogs at such a young age. Thank you to my Uncle Peter Zaphiris for inspiring my love of nature and outdoor exploration. Life is a treasure hunt.

Thank you to my beloved and most special dog, Django. Thank you to my three, living, wonderful dogs, Eugene (back cover), Mega-Man (cover shot), and C. Bean.